The University of Maryland at College Park, A History

George H. Callcott

Noble House
Baltimore, Maryland

The University of Maryland at College Park, A History

Library of Congress
Cataloging-in-Publication Data
ISBN 1-56167-889-9

Library of Congress Card Catalog Number:
2005920495

Published by

8019 Belair Road, Suite 10
Baltimore, Maryland 21236

Manufactured in the United States of America

Contents

Preface

Forty years ago, young and brash, I wrote a history of this institution at which I had just arrived. Now, brash and older, I am writing again about the institution I will soon be leaving. This is a revision of my earlier history, plus an account of the years since it appeared. Mostly it is about the past, but it is also my effort to understand what is happening in universities nowadays—their aims and attainments, their administration and finance, the changes taking places in the disciplines and professional schools, and the changes in faculty and student culture.

Two years ago, President C. D. Mote, Jr. and Vice President William W. Destler encouraged me to undertake this project, and I expected the University of Maryland to publish it. More recently, however, officials in University Relations grew skittish, fearful that any narrative of the past that was published by the University would be considered an official statement. I have proceeded, therefore, with another publisher, and the University need feel no responsibility.

Many people have aided me. Robert Berdhal, Ira Berlin, George E. Dieter, J. Robert Dorfman, Irwin L. Goldstein, James H. Lesher, Anne S. K. Turkos, and my wife Peggy read all or parts of the manuscript and offered advice. Anne, especially, along with members of her staff in University Archives, checked and corrected facts, approved or criticized almost every word of text, and helped in obtaining the pictures. To all of these, I express appreciation and absolve them from blame. This remains a personal selection of facts that I believe are important or interesting, and my opinions about them.

George H. Callcott
January 2005

CHAPTER I

Before College Park

The Maryland Agricultural College at College Park was founded in 1856 and became a university in 1920, but the desire for a university had been growing for centuries.

The very discovery of the new world had inspired dreamers. Philosophers like Thomas More and Francis Bacon were planning universities for the new land before the first settlers arrived, and the first actual attempt to found a college in the British colonies occurred in what is now Maryland. By the time of the American Revolution, backwoods America had more colleges and a higher literacy rate, even counting its slaves, than any country in the world.

The first English college in America was the quixotic scheme of Edward Palmer, a wealthy English barrister who had attended Oxford University and was an investor in the London Company that financed the first English settlement at Jamestown in 1607. In 1616, Palmer persuaded the Company to give him title to an island in the Susquehanna River, just outside the present town of Havre de Grace, for the specific purpose of building a college that would be modeled after Oxford. It was probably intended less as an educational institution than as a refuge for scholars and artists. A few years later, probably in 1622, the university founders established a settlement, or at least a camp, on Palmer's Island. This was still ten years before Maryland was separated from Virginia, ten years before the first permanent settlement in Maryland. Actually, we know very little about the failed scheme, except that Palmer wrote that he had been "at many thousand pounds expense" in his efforts, and a few years later, English vessels found the remains of a settlement on Palmer's Island, including some abandoned books. Here was a dream of the future—the first university in America—and a story that should be better known.

Even when the early efforts failed, the ambition for colleges surged

3

on. Elsewhere in the English colonies, the Puritans established Harvard in 1636, just six years after landing; Virginia established William and Mary in 1693; and by 1789—when the colonies became a nation and when England still had but two universities—the little frontier society boasted twenty-four institutions of higher learning, and two of them were in Maryland.

Maryland's first two lasting institutions of higher learning were Washington College of Chestertown, founded in 1782, and St. John's College of Annapolis, founded in 1784, combined under a single chancellor as the state-supported University of Maryland. The founder and chancellor was William Smith, a contentious Scotsman and an Anglican clergyman. Benjamin Franklin had chosen him to serve as principle of the academy that eventually became the University of Pennsylvania. As an academic leader, he was brilliantly successful, but he was soon in trouble for his flamboyant opinions—his support of education of Native Americans, his hatred of France, his opposition to American independence from England. Twice, while he was president at Pennsylvania, he also served in jail. As the American Revolution ended, he found his way to Maryland, opened an academy in Chestertown, and petitioned the General Assembly to make it into a university. The Assembly agreed, provided that he would raise 5,000 pounds sterling in gifts and that he would open a similar institution on the

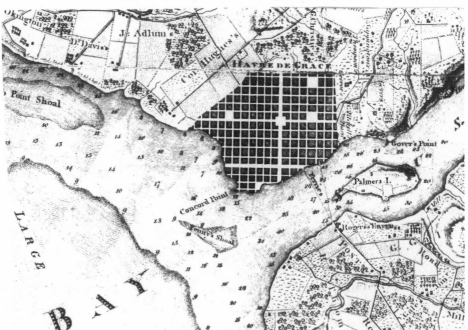

1. Palmer's Island, now known as Garrett Island, outside the town of Havre de Grace, site of the first university in the English colonies. C.P. Hauducoeur map of 1799.

2. William Smith, 1727-1803, founded Washington College in 1782 and St. John's College in 1784. He combined them as the University of Maryland and became its first chancellor.

Western Shore of the Chesapeake. Smith quickly met the conditions, and the General Assembly approved his charter. The State provided an annual appropriation of 3,500 pounds sterling for operating expenses. It also exempted faculty and students from all state taxes.

As long as Smith was in charge, both institutions thrived. The chancellor created two courses of study, one emphasizing classics for students aspiring to be clergymen or lawyers, and another—far ahead of its time—emphasizing modern languages, sciences, and accounting—for students intending to be merchants or farmers. But then, in 1789, as all was going well, Smith resigned in hopes of being elected the first bishop of the new American Episcopal Church. He was defeated for bishop, probably because of his reputation for too strong language and too much drink. The chancellor's office fell vacant, and state support dwindled away. If the two institutions had remained as a university with state support, they would have constituted the first state university in America, and the first state university system. Instead, the board of trustees divided, one group for each institution. The colleges went their own way, successful enough as private institutions, each continuing through the centuries to produce a considerable portion of the state's leadership.

The University of Maryland at College Park, A History

Elementary and secondary education in Maryland still depended on private initiatives, and those initiatives were many. Children mostly learned to read from their mothers or from female relatives, and families often joined together to hire tutors. Occasionally the state, or a county or a church, contributed, here and there, to maintain a boarding academy. In England, for all its maturity and wealth, the adult literacy rate was around 30 percent in 1800; but in Maryland, where almost a third of the population were slaves, literacy for all its adult inhabitants was about 45 percent. Approximately two percent of Maryland's adult population received some form of higher education—either from the two colleges in Maryland, from neighboring states, or from abroad. Of course, all of those with higher education were male.

During the nineteenth century, the passion for education soared on. Maryland's first public school system began in Baltimore in 1829, and the first high school opened ten years later. By the Civil War, free schools had spread to every county, although they were still out of reach for most rural families. Adult literacy in Maryland rose to around 60 percent. State leaders, however, still assumed that education came from the top down, from colleges to public schools, and the greatest efforts of public funding and private philanthropy went into universities and colleges.

Every section of the state wanted a college, every religious denomination, every profession. By 1860, the Maryland General Assembly had approved charters for twenty additional four-year colleges, in order of founding: Cokesbury, Baltimore, Mount St. Mary's, University College of Arts and Sciences, Asbury, Maryland, Frederick, Franklin, Mount Hope, St. James, New Windsor, Newton, Baltimore Female, St. Charles, Loyola, Calvert, Maryland Agricultural, Mount Washington Female, Irving, Borromeo. Most of the colleges lasted only a few years, but some remain. By far the most important was the Maryland Agricultural College. In addition to these four-year colleges, nine professional colleges appeared, in order: St. Mary's Seminary, the College of Medicine, College of Divinity, College of Law, Institute for Mechanic Arts, Washington Medical College, Baltimore Dental College, College of Pharmacy, and the United States Naval Academy. The most important of the professional colleges, along with the Naval Academy, was the College of Medicine of Maryland of 1807. Five years later, the College of Medicine became the University of Maryland, and over time it created or absorbed the Colleges of Arts and Sciences, Law, Divinity, Dentistry, and Pharmacy. In 1920, the University of Maryland, all in Baltimore, merged with the Maryland Agricultural College in College Park.

Before College Park

The professional institutions were different from traditional colleges. The colleges stemmed from an English tradition—usually in a rural setting, residential, with stern discipline, a classical and religious curriculum, dedicated to building moral character. The professional institutions, on the other hand, stemmed from a Scottish-Continental tradition—in an urban setting, for day students, with a curriculum that provided practical training and a license to practice a profession. The professional schools emerged as the professions matured, as master practitioners took on apprentices, and as trained practitioners distinguished themselves from their untrained competitors. Maryland, with its large Baltimore urban center, offered special leadership in professional education—the sixth medical school in America, the third law school, the first dental school, and the fourth school of pharmacy.

The founder of the College of Medicine was John Beale Davidge, a shy and scholarly physician, one of the first graduates of St. John's College. He had obtained an M.D. and advanced training from the universities in Glasgow and Edinburgh, and he was revered by his colleagues in Baltimore. Eager to extend his own knowledge, especially of anatomy, and followed by admiring apprentices, he acquired cadavers wherever he could, asking too few questions of his suppliers. His neighbors, suspicious and superstitious, stormed his laboratory. His colleagues, in turn, stormed to his defense, and in 1807, they obtained from the General Assembly an act incorporating Davidge and five other physicians as a College of Medicine.

Joining Davidge's faculty was prestigious and profitable, and his professors were distinguished. Davidge took the chair of surgery, and others assumed chairs of anatomy, chemistry, pharmacy, practice, and obstetrics. The faculty governed themselves, collecting fees from the students and sharing the proceeds. Students paid about $140 for the academic year that lasted from October to March, and two such years completed their study. The degree they received placed them immediately among the most respected—and best-paid—physicians of Maryland or of any state.

The institution was so successful—both in raising the standard of medical care and in profits for its graduates—that other professions were eager to follow. In 1812, the General Assembly authorized the College of Medicine to change its name to the University of Maryland. Medicine would constitute one of the University's colleges, and new faculties would be created to offer degrees in law, divinity, and arts and sciences. To encourage the institution, the General Assembly authorized the University to conduct at least three state lotteries, which, after expenses, eventually netted over $69,000.

The College of Medicine profited most from the lottery. The professors built themselves a magnificent building, quite the finest American medical structure of its day. Designed by Maximilian Godefroy and Robert Carey Long, it was a pantheon-like structure, built around two vast operating theatres. Today it remains the center of the medical campus. A few years later, the College added a teaching hospital and pioneered in clinical instruction. Its faculty, some attracted from Europe, was among the best anywhere. By the Civil War, it was graduating about sixty physicians each year, and the public had almost accepted the medical college degree as the basis for legitimate practice.

The University's College of Law, founded in 1812, was almost equally successful. Its dean was David Hoffman, generally recognized at the time as the state's outstanding attorney and able to recruit to his faculty some of the finest attorneys in Maryland and nearby states. Hoffman's greatest contribution was his treatise, *A Course of Legal Study* (1817), the first significant legal textbook in the United States. Reviewers observed that Hoffman had codified the study of law much as Sir William Blackstone in the previous century had codified the law itself. Hoffman's categories of study—property rights, personal rights, equity, criminal law, business law, and the rest, along with his lists of required readings and moot court de-

3. The College of Medicine of Maryland, founded in 1807, became the University of Maryland in 1812.

sign—set the pattern that prevailed over the country for the next half century. There was a downside to the book's success, however, for students throughout the country could use his textbook and his published lectures on their own without paying fees to hear a professor read them aloud. The College produced about fifteen graduates each year, many moving into positions of judicial and political leadership, but still a majority of students in Maryland, as elsewhere, read for the bar and practiced without a degree.

Other colleges within the University did less well. The College of Divinity foundered because of denominational rivalries. The College of Arts and Sciences produced a few graduates but eventually faded away because parents were not ready for nonresident undergraduate education, and student fees did not adequately support a faculty.

Briefly, from 1826 to 1839, the state attempted to take over the privately operated University of Maryland to transform it into what would have been the seventh state university in the country, with a college for undergraduates at its core. The faculties in the professional schools mostly opposed the takeover, however, and the effort collapsed. The state would have to wait and look elsewhere—to College Park—for a state-supported college for undergraduates.

Meanwhile, the dentists of Maryland wanted scientific education, along with the credentialing that degrees provided. In 1841, Horace H. Hayden and Chapin A. Harris created the first dental school in America—the first in the world—and a model for those to come. It is fair to say that the profession of modern dentistry originated here in Maryland. That same year, a group of pharmacists in the state organized to create a College of Pharmacy, the fourth such college in the country. The College of Dentistry and the College of Pharmacy both began separately from the University, but the University was supportive and eventually absorbed them. The professional schools—Medicine, Law, Dentistry, and Pharmacy—were all proprietary, owned by the faculty and dependent entirely on student fees. This meant that the faculty was actually selling its degrees, and standards depended mainly on faculty dedication and cohesion. Until about the time of the Civil War, the system worked, but it was bound to fail eventually, as faculty diverted student fees for equipment into personal income, as quarrels divided the faculty, and as competing schools sprang up to offer ever-easier degrees for ever-lower fees.

By the time of the Civil War, Maryland's total educational system was a mix of successes and failures. Maryland's state support for public schools lagged behind all the states to the north, although its literacy rate was about the same as in other states and far ahead of Europe. Maryland's state support for colleges lagged behind all the states to the south, although it had a multitude of private colleges, far more than it needed, and its professional schools were, for the moment, among the best in America.

Meanwhile, the Maryland Agricultural College at College Park was just emerging as a rather traditional residential college, mainly for farmer's sons. Its founders imagined, however, that it was also a professional school, dedicated to research and to a transformation of the state's economy. Its founders imagined—as founders were wont to do—that they had hit upon the educational system of the future.

CHAPTER II

The Founding of the Maryland Agricultural College

The cities and the urban professions were surging ahead in the 1850s, but still the great majority of the people in Maryland lived on the farm. The Maryland Agricultural College was an attempt to rescue this huge but declining way of life.

Tobacco had been the source of Maryland's eighteenth-century golden age, but after the American Revolution, and especially after the War of 1812, Europe turned to Turkey and Egypt for its weed. The price of Maryland's leading crop dropped from twenty cents a pound in 1810 to five cents in 1850. Farm values plunged; five rural counties had a smaller population in 1850 than a half-century before; and a third of the children born on Maryland farms were leaving the state. Still, however, there were rich planters aplenty, and they took the lead in the search for recovery.

Some farmers, blaming their plight on the state's support for business, talked of the rural counties seceding from the state. Others, blaming the northern states for tariffs and for anti-slave agitation, talked of Maryland seceding from the country. Still others imagined that the solution to the farmer's plight lay in education—scientific research, better farming techniques, new crops, new fertilizers, and new farm machinery. They spoke of the industrial revolution followed by an agricultural revolution.

Farmers everywhere shared the frustration and search for solutions, but Maryland, which was at the forefront of the agricultural decline, was also a leader in a search for its revival. In 1785, a Marylander in Philadelphia founded the country's first agricultural society where farmers organized to share information, and by 1860, there were nearly a thousand such societies over the country. In 1809, Marylanders living in the District of Columbia helped organize the first agricultural fair where farmers came to display their wares, learn about the successful techniques of their

11

neighbors, and admire the new farm machinery. Soon the fairs were an American tradition. Farm journals proliferated, and one of the first and finest was John Skinner's *American Farmer*, published in Baltimore.

The societies, the orators at the county fairs, and the agricultural journals together persuaded the Maryland General Assembly in 1832 to appoint a state geologist to search for decayed seashells, or marl, to be used as fertilizer for the farms. A few years later, the Assembly appointed a state chemist to test commercial fertilizers. But these were baby steps toward agricultural revival. Increasingly, the societies, the orators, and the journals looked toward agricultural education as the way forward.

The major impetus for the Maryland Agricultural College was the aristocratic Baltimore Farmer's Club, later renamed the Maryland State Agricultural Society. Only the wealthiest planters belonged, paying the high initiation fees and traveling to the club's posh facility in Baltimore, where they sat in leather chairs, drank Maryland rye whiskey, and discussed the affairs of the day. They talked about a college where their sons could learn gentlemanly values and engage in scientific research, or, alternatively, of a vocational school where their slovenly, poorer neighbors could learn to work harder. Their aims alternated and merged.

The leader in these discussions was Charles Benedict Calvert, one of the wealthiest and easily the most aristocratic of its members. Ultimately it was his college. As surely as Thomas Jefferson, Johns Hopkins, or James B. Duke established universities that became famous, Charles Calvert was the founder of the Maryland Agricultural College that became the University of Maryland at College Park.

Charles Calvert was the seven-times great-grandson of the founder of the Maryland colony and a relative of six Maryland governors. He grew up at Riversdale, a plantation house still standing, mostly restored, just over a mile south of the present campus. His father, George, was a respected planter who served from time to time in the General Assembly. His mother, Rosalie, who wrote eloquently of their life at Riversdale, was the daughter of a Belgian aristocrat who fled the French Revolution. Charles entered the University of Virginia in 1826, just one year after it opened, and, for two years, he studied the traditional curriculum of classics and philosophy. Probably, like most entering students, Charles visited Monticello and dined with Thomas Jefferson, although Jefferson died that summer. If they had dined together, Jefferson must have spoken of his desire, expressed while he was president, to visit Riversdale, but Charles's mother, who disapproved of Jefferson's politics, had pointedly withheld the invitation. Charles disliked his classmate, Edgar Allan Poe, whom he

4. Charles B. Calvert, 1808-1864, founder of the Maryland Agricultural College. Photograph by Matthew Brady.

considered bohemian and a troublemaker. After two years in Charlottesville, Charles returned home, eventually took over the management of Riversdale, and, with his mother's fortune, he made it into a model plantation. The agricultural journals of the day lavished attention on Riversdale. By the 1850s, its fame as a model plantation had quite outdistanced its Virginia rivals, Mount Vernon and Monticello.

In front of Riversdale were entry gates with a porter's lodge; a mile-long drive led to the mansion. Behind it was a lake with an artificial island on which stood a Chinese pagoda. Around the lake were terraces, fountains, arbors, and greenhouses. Behind Riversdale, some distance away, was an immense hexagonal barn, which a reporter called the finest barn in America. The farm itself was devoted mainly to grain and dairy operations, although Calvert was constantly experimenting with new crops and animal breeds, with irrigation, fertilizers, and new farm machinery.

By 1856, Charles Calvert owned about 1,900 acres (three square miles), stretching along the turnpike, now Route One, from Riversdale to what is now the Capital Beltway. To the west were slightly smaller plantations belonging to Robert Clark, who lived at Hitching Post Hill, and Colonel Robert O. Eversfield, who lived near the modern University president's house. Eventually the University absorbed parts of these lands.

The labor on Calvert's plantation was mostly slave, of course, and in subsequent years that would cast a shadow over everything that Calvert built, including the college. Like George Washington and Thomas Jefferson, he was painfully aware of its brutality. He was aware that his

5. The Riversdale Plantation in 1827.

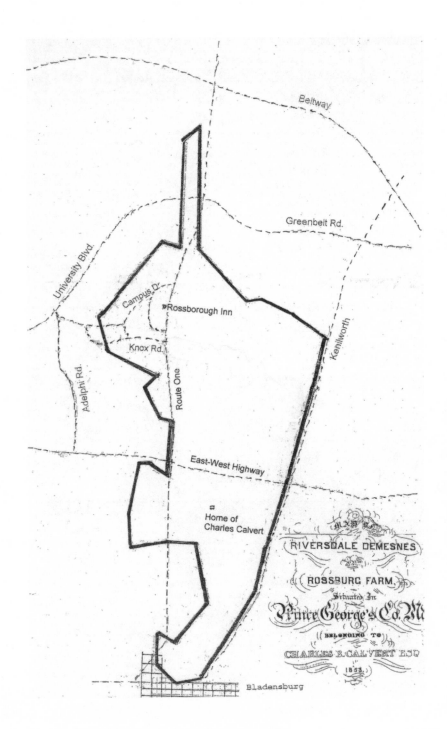

6. A map of Riversdale in 1853, shown with modern roads.

father had a slave mistress and that he himself had half-brothers and half-sisters who were born into slavery and then freed. Calvert brooded about slavery and did not like to discuss it. He reduced his slave holdings from about fifty when his father died, to about twenty when the Civil War came, and probably—we do not know for certain—he freed them all as the war proceeded, just before he died in 1864. Still, he never publicly denounced slavery, and we must live with that.

Calvert recruited the ablest leaders in Maryland for his college-building scheme. From the Eastern Shore came James T. Earle, William T. Goldsborough, and John C. Groome; from Southern Maryland, John S. Skinner, Nicholas B. Worthington, Robert Bowie, John H. Southron, Allen Bowie Davis, and William N. Mercer; from around Baltimore, Thomas Swann, Charles Carroll, and John Merryman; and from the western counties, John O. Wharton, Thomas Perry, and George R. Dennis. Most were planters. All were major stockholders in the new institution. The movement for the college came not from small farmers, but from large planters—both generous and self-serving—who wanted to educate their own sons and the sons of their well-off neighbors.

On March 6, 1856, the General Assembly agreed that, provided the

7. The trustees sold $50,000 worth of stock to raise money for the new college. The stock split several times but never paid a dividend. This certificate was issued to Charles Calvert.

16

trustees raise $50,000, the Maryland Agricultural College should be incorporated, with the right to offer degrees, and that the institution would be provided with a state appropriation of $6,000 a year. Token opposition to the bill came from representatives of small farmers who feared rich planter domination, but urban delegates were pleased to support the college as a sop to the ever-complaining planters. Maryland chartered the third agricultural college in America. The institutions that became Pennsylvania State University and Michigan State University began one year earlier.

To raise the $50,000, the trustees sold stock at $25 a share. They encouraged the hope that dividends might eventually result from the student fees they would collect and from profits from the new crops they would develop, but most stockholders knew their investment was gratuitous. The largest stockholder, with 300 shares, was William Mercer, a once-bankrupt Maryland tobacco farmer who had moved to Louisiana to make a fortune in sugar. Calvert was next with 176 shares. W. W. Corcoran, the Washington banker who founded the Corcoran Gallery of Art, bought 40 shares, and Johns Hopkins in Baltimore, who was developing an interest in higher education, bought 20 shares. The shareholders elected a board of trustees to purchase land for the college, erect buildings, determine a course of study, and employ a faculty. Calvert was elected chairman of the board, and Dr. John O. Wharton, a graduate of the College of Medicine, became the first employee, the executive secretary of the board and the college registrar, at a salary of $1,000 annually.

The first question was where the college should be located. One stockholder offered 100 acres in Montgomery County as an outright gift. Others offered farms at discount rates. As usual, however, Calvert topped the offers. He would provide 428 acres of his own model plantation for $50 an acre, or $21,400—an excellent price for land so near a railroad—and then he would provide $10,000 toward this payment in the form of an indefinite loan without interest. Eventually he waived payment altogether.

This land, on which the campus now stands, was already rich in history. Native Americans had roamed the land—excavations for campus buildings still uncover their artifacts. In 1688, an Englishman, William Middleton, paid 20 pounds sterling for 123 acres along Paint Branch and named it "Godfather's Gift." Middleton's son, Robert, added 600 acres more, built a cabin, girdled some trees, and planted some corn to eat and some tobacco to sell. He floated the casks of tobacco down Paint Branch to Bladensburg to be loaded onto ships bound for England. The land changed hands often, always in large packets—to Arthur Nelson, to Benjamin Belt (who gave his name to Beltsville), on through various owners to Richard Ross, and on to Calvert.

Ross was a tavern keeper in Bladensburg, excited by the prospect that Washington was about to become the national capital and keenly aware that this property provided the main route to the north. Ross bought the land for $15 an acre, and, in 1804, he completed an inn, called Rossborough. Tax assessors considered it the eighth most valuable structure in the county, much below George Calvert's new Riversdale, just over a mile to the south, and just below Thomas Snowden's Montpelier in Laurel. The inn received its most famous visitor in 1824 when General Lafayette, the French hero of the American Revolution, on a grand tour of the United States, stopped there overnight. The next morning, President James Monroe came to escort him into Washington. Two centuries later, the inn remains—much restored but nowadays in nearly its original form—as the University's Faculty Club.

Ross joined with George Calvert, the father of Charles Calvert, and with others to create the Washington-Baltimore Turnpike Corporation, which improved the road, established tollbooths every ten miles, and charged about one cent per mile for every carriage that traveled from one booth to the next. For a while the turnpike prospered, but it ceased collecting tolls after about 1840 when the railroad came. Ross moved on. Charles Calvert acquired the land.

Once the trustees selected the site, construction of the main college buildings proceeded rapidly. Charles Calvert was there on horseback every day, supervising everything, sometimes bringing his slaves to help the contractors. The founders were growing excited. "We will," said Calvert, "have the best Institution *in the world.*"

The campus was impressive, immediately the finest campus in the state. The main building—known as the Barracks—was an ivory-colored, brick structure, five stories high, Gothic in style, located in a grove of trees on the highest hill, where LeFrak Hall now stands. On the first floor was an auditorium that doubled as a dining hall, plus kitchen facilities and a huge bathroom with iron tubs that people considered very modern. On the second floor were eight carpeted lecture rooms and some offices. On each of the top three floors were eighteen rooms, 12 by 23 feet, each furnished with two beds and two wardrobes—quarters for 108 students, although sometimes two of the rooms were combined as quarters for a professor. The building had steam heat, and a machine in the rear of the building turned coal into gas that was pumped into every room for lights.

There were three other buildings. Calvert converted the Rossborough

8. The Baltimore-Washington Turnpike, with stagecoaches and inns along the way, prospered from about 1800 to the 1830s, when the railroad came. This picture was drawn just north of the Rossborough Inn.

9. The railroad from Baltimore to Washington opened in 1834. This drawing was made near Riversdale a few years later.

Inn into a home for the registrar and headquarters for the experimental farm. He built a new president's house, of frame with fashionable gingerbread decoration, located where the Health Center now stands. An identical house for a professor was located behind the present-day College Park shopping center. Other professors had rooms in the main building with the students or lived off-campus. The campus was nicely landscaped, with roads and newly planted shrubbery. Just south of the main building, Calvert planted an orchard with a wide variety of fruit trees. Near the road were fifty-seven plots of land, carefully marked off by cords, where he was testing nineteen varieties of fertilizer.

More difficult than construction of a beautiful campus were the searches for the college's exact mission, for a president and faculty, and for students. The trustees quickly shunted aside the notion of a vocational school for ordinary farmers and instead embraced the idea of a more traditional college for their own sons. The college would provide some emphasis on science, and the boys would work after classes under the farm director on experimental crops, but actually there was really not much scientific agriculture to be taught. This problem of formulating an institutional mission was to rankle for half a century.

The trustees also found it hard to obtain a suitable president and faculty. For president, they turned finally to Benjamin Hallowell, a fine Quaker schoolmaster living in Montgomery County, Maryland, noted

10. The original plan for the Maryland Agricultural College. Only the wing on the left was completed, still one of the finest college buildings in the country.

for his lectures on scientific agriculture, but not a college graduate himself. Hallowell let it be known that he disapproved of slavery, and the trustees, to their credit, accepted that, forbidding the college from owning or hiring slaves. In addition to serving as president, Hallowell also was to teach English, history, philosophy, and Christianity. A second professor taught ancient and modem languages, and a third taught mathematics and engineering. A fourth taught what the catalogue called agricultural sciences, but this meant chemistry, physics, geology, and botany.

Opening ceremonies for the College, October 6, 1859, were glittering. Some 250 people arrived by train from Baltimore, another 250 came by train from Washington, and 250 more came by carriage from the surrounding countryside. At least two United States senators, a Supreme Court justice, and a presidential cabinet member attended. Calvert presided over the ceremonies, of course. Joseph Henry, head of the new Smithsonian Institution, was the main speaker of the day, lauding what he supposed was the union of higher education with scientific research, but a union far from established. Calvert provided a sumptuous picnic for everyone. Enrollment that first day was disappointing, only thirty-four students struggling in through the crowds. Most were sons of the trustees or of other prominent planter families. During the year, another fifteen or so students drifted in.

Hallowell lasted for only a month—he said the boys gave him headaches—and for the rest of the year, Calvert took over as acting president.

11. The Barracks, completed in 1859, burned in 1912.

Calvert hired someone else to teach English, history, philosophy, and Christianity, and he engaged a prominent Washington scientist, Townsend Glover, to teach botany and entomology. It was probably the first entomology course taught in America. For the second year, Calvert hired the principal of a local academy, John M. Colby, to serve as president—three presidents in two years. The faculty came and went almost as often.

As in most colleges of the day, education began with discipline and religion. The College would build character in the boys, even if their fathers had failed. The rules were long, beginning with prohibitions on "loud talking, scuffling, boisterous behavior, or unnecessary noise of any kind." Other rules prohibited students from bringing guns or gunpowder to the campus and forbade "attempts to injure any member of the Faculty, in his person." Absences from class or campus were forbidden, except that every five weeks, if a student's behavior was perfect, he might apply for permission to leave the campus at noon Saturday and return by sunup Monday. After discipline came religion. Each morning the students assembled to hear the president or one of the professors lead prayers and read scripture. During the day, a professor said grace before each meal. Every Sunday, a visiting preacher from a different denomination conducted services.

The classroom routine was similar to most colleges, with about six hours of recitation each day. The trustees were especially pleased, however, with their solution to the problem of physical fitness for the boys. Instead of gymnastics or wasteful athletic competition, each student was to spend at least one hour each afternoon working under the direction of Dr. John Wharton on the College farm. This would dignify labor, provide exercise, sap the students' energy for delinquency, and profit the farm. Other outdoor assignments were still more imaginative. Each student was to plant a group of trees, shrubs, or flowers to beautify the campus. He would then tend his plot throughout his college career and be judged on the result. One group of students was assigned responsibility for providing ice throughout the year, by constructing a pond and building an icehouse. Another group was responsible for constructing strawberry beds that would provide desserts.

The College, like most in the country, generally shielded students from current events. Intellectual life, besides the memorized lessons, seemed almost to be an extracurricular activity. Most students belonged to either the Mercer Literary Society or the Calvert Fraternity, and rivalry was keen between the two. Each society had a library. Members met weekly to hear invited outside speakers, to offer orations to the neighborhood on their views, or to debate the issues of the day. The issue of slavery was off-limits even in the literary societies. One evening, the Mercer Society debated, "Are the mental faculties of the sexes equal?" and, after the debate, the members voted in the negative.

College enrollment held steady during the second year, but faculty turnover was high, and the first commencement was still to come. The campus was handsome, its finances adequate, and, while other institutions received occasional contributions from the state, this was the only college receiving a regular state appropriation. The planters of Maryland had created for themselves a mostly traditional college—traditional in its small size, its elitist enrollment, its curriculum, its routine. Their dream of a new kind of a practical education, of scientific agriculture, of elevating the farmers of the state, had hardly materialized. Their dream would remain, but the day of the planter was almost over.

CHAPTER III

The Civil War

When the Civil War began, most people in Maryland sympathized with the South, but by the time it ended, they mostly embraced emancipation and the Union. As the war wound down, people were looking for more democratic kinds of education than had existed before the war. The little agricultural college was caught between its Southern elitist past and its Northern democratic future.

The College was only in its second year when the sectional conflict erupted into war. Each day, faculty and students awaited the latest news. There was no telegraph or direct mail to the College, but each morning someone rode on horseback down to the railroad tracks where the trains now stopped regularly at "College Station." By dinner time, which was two o'clock, the professors had picked up their newspapers and mail from the president's office, and, even though the faculty attempted to withhold it, the day's news filtered down among the students.

Early in the fall of 1860, soon after classes began that second year, word came of Lincoln's election. In December came the news that South Carolina had seceded, and in January 1861, six other states left the Union. In February, as Lincoln went through Baltimore on the way to his inauguration, there were riots in the city. Then, April 12, came the biggest news of all—Confederate forces had fired on Fort Sumter. Within a week, Lincoln called for volunteers, and Virginia, just ten miles away from the College, severed its ties with the Union. Maryland was in turmoil, with troops everywhere. Governor Thomas Hicks resolutely refused to allow the General Assembly to convene, for a majority of the delegates were ready to join the Confederacy.

With each news bulletin, more students and faculty drifted away from the College. At least twenty students and one professor joined the army or navy of the Confederacy; at least nine students went off to fight for the Union. The fall term of 1860 had begun with forty-three students and six professors, but the academic year ended with seventeen students and three faculty.

Still the College struggled on. The third year, 1861-1862, began with about twenty-five students and still another new president, the fourth in three years. He was Henry Onderdonk, a Quaker schoolmaster, quite able. Troops now moved regularly along the road in front of the College, and there were rumors that the College would be taken over as a Union training camp or hospital. Still the recitations went on. Prices of farm products were high, and for the first time, the College farm was turning a profit.

At the end of the third year, July 1862, the College offered its first two degrees, an A.B. degree to William B. Sands, who had taken mostly Latin and philosophy, and a B.S. degree to Thomas Franklin, who had concentrated on the new science courses. Despite the war, graduation festivities were sparkling, with parties, orations, and a ball that lasted all night. The following year, there were two more graduates, and in 1864, there were three, or possibly four.

In April 1864, Union General Ambrose E. Burnside, moving from Annapolis to Washington, camped his 6,000 troops on the College grounds. The troops destroyed some fences, and the College sued the government in vain for damages. Three months later, Confederate General Bradley T. Johnson, a Marylander, swept through with at least 400 men, threatening

12. In April, 1861, Union troops passed through Baltimore, and the city erupted in riots.

13. As classes began in 1862, over 5,000 men were dying at nearby Antietam.

14. In July, 1864, General Bradley T. Johnson, from Frederick, Maryland, and his 400 Confederate troops spent the night on the campus, where College officials welcomed them warmly.

Washington from the rear. On July 11, Johnson set up headquarters in the Rossborough Inn, and his men camped around it. Students and officials at the College welcomed them warmly. That evening, College officials provided food for the soldiers, and young women appeared from the surrounding neighborhood. Fifes and fiddles came out, and partying lasted into the night. The troops left the next morning, but for months Union officials were investigating who had supplied the invaders and exactly what had happened that evening. Public anger at the College's expression of Southern sympathy lasted for many years.

The storm over the affair forced Onderdonk to resign. During 1864-1865 and 1865-1866, the College, with one or two professors, struggled along, operating mainly as a prep school for boys age 12 or older. To meet expenses, the trustees sold off 200 acres of land, now the College Park shopping area and College Heights Estates. In the fall of 1866, the College failed to open. The farm continued with hired labor, but, for the moment, the planters' dream seemed to have died, a casualty of the war. Tentatively, haltingly, it reopened in March 1867, with four professors and sixteen students.

While the College foundered, however, the idea of agricultural education was emerging anew, this time from a very different direction, but again Charles Calvert was in the forefront. In 1860, with the College underway, Calvert ran for Congress and was elected as a Unionist—a party with a peculiar platform, pro-Union and also pro-slave. Seldom had a first-term Congressman made such an impression. First, he was a leading spokesman for federal compensation for freed or runaway slaves, which was a means of gradually ending slavery and ending the war as well. People listened, but of course the idea failed. Second, to promote agricultural interests, Calvert was an ardent advocate of a bill to establish a United States Department of Agriculture. The bill passed, creating a Bureau of Agriculture that later became a cabinet department. Third, he was one of the main supporters of the land grant act, for which Justin Morrill of Vermont was the first sponsor.

The land grant act, passed in 1862, provided that each state would receive 30,000 acres of federal lands in the west for each congressman and senator. Each state was to use the proceeds to endow a college that would emphasize agriculture, engineering, and military tactics. The agricultural emphasis was to court farmers, who were often skeptical of the war for union; engineering was to provide the army with officers who could build railroads; and military tactics, added at the last moment, was to help win the War. In Maryland, the Maryland Agricultural College was the obvious recipient. The state impatiently sold its entire tract for 53 ½ cents an acre, a total of $112,504. A few years later, the value would have increased tenfold. The money was invested in bonds that paid the institution about $4,500 annually.

The land grant act was a milestone in the development of American democracy. It was a bridge between higher education and the needs of the people, a means for ordinary people—farmers and artisans—to obtain an inexpensive education in new and practical subjects. Here was the focus for which the founders of the Maryland Agricultural College were reaching and never quite grasped. Today, there are 105 land grant colleges and universities in the United States, and their impact has been larger than even Morrill and Calvert imagined.

War and reconstruction inspired other dreamers. Libertus Van Bokkelen was an Episcopal priest in Baltimore and an ardent crusader for public schools. In 1864, when Maryland called a constitutional convention to abolish slavery, Van Bokkelen descended on the convention to press his plan for a state school system capped by a state university. The delegates, awash in wartime idealism, embraced the plan, and the governor named Van Bokkelen superintendent of public schools and chancellor of higher education. The public school system lasts today with state support for elementary and secondary schools in every county, to serve people of all races, and with new teachers' colleges to supply the system with staff.

Although Van Bokkelen's system for higher education lasted little more than a year, from 1865 into 1867, it anticipated the statewide system of higher education that emerged a century later. According to the plan, almost all of higher education was to be united as the state-supported University of Maryland—the professional schools of Baltimore, Washington and St. John's Colleges, and the Maryland Agricultural College. Van Bokkelen himself would serve as chancellor and advocate. The plan collapsed when the Baltimore professional schools withdrew, unwilling to exchange their fee income for state salaries. Then Washington and St. John's withdrew when the chancellor declined to assume responsibility for their debts. The Maryland Agricultural College agreed halfheartedly to state affiliation, allowing the state to appoint four of its eleven trustees in exchange for minuscule funding. As a state system, however, or even transforming the Maryland Agricultural College into a full-fledged state university, Van Bokkelen had failed. The failures to build a state university were mounting: in 1622, 1784, 1826, and 1865.

The Civil War, like all revolutions, had destroyed much and promised

15. In 1865, Libertus Van Bokkelen combined four Maryland colleges into a University of Maryland System.

much. Slavery and the planter class were gone, and rural power and rural values were in decline. The Maryland Agricultural College was shuttered, at least for the moment, caught between the past and future. Still, there was promise ahead. A new democracy prevailed, and grandiose ideas like those of Justin Morrill and Libertus Van Bokkelen reached out even to the farmer. The Maryland Agricultural College was the only institution in the state with both federal and state support, and it would eventually find its way.

CHAPTER IV

Seeking a Mission, 1867-1892

For twenty-five years, from reopening in 1867 until 1892 when federal money became plentiful, the Maryland Agricultural College struggled on—a lonely little college up there on the hill, looking for its mission.

In education, as in everything else, the growth and excitement of the Gilded Age was mostly in the cities. Maryland farms declined from 57 percent of the state wealth in 1860 to barely 33 percent in 1900; the average farm size declined from 190 acres to 113 acres. In Baltimore, meanwhile, the population more than doubled, wealth more than tripled, and the public school movement was catching on. In higher education, the great Johns Hopkins University opened in 1876 with an income from endowment that was forty times what the Maryland Agricultural College received from the state. The University of Maryland professional schools in Baltimore were booming in size if not in quality, and at least four other colleges in Baltimore boasted enrollments larger than that at College Park.

The Agricultural College still lacked—as it had in Calvert's day—much of anything to teach about the farm beyond what a boy could learn from his father. Calvert was content to begin with botany and entomology in hopes these basic sciences would grow into something practical. Other land grant colleges—Cornell, Wisconsin, California—were beginning in the same way. But so far, even at the most prosperous institutions, results were meager. For the first twenty-five years, the land grant colleges were mostly failures in finding much of anything that was useful to teach about agriculture.

The Maryland Agricultural College struggled on, looking for a purpose—(1) as a traditional college, emphasizing classics and science, for the sons of gentlemen; (2) then primarily as a school for instruction in Christian morality, (3) then mainly as an engineering school that helped farmers' sons escape the farm, or (4) as a military school, and (5) finally as an institution dedicated to agricultural services. Seven college presidents during 25 years mixed these goals and alternated among them:

Presidents and Their Missions, 1867-1892

President	Background	Mission	Dates
Charles L. C. Minor	Captain, CSA	Classics, Science	1867-1868
Franklin Buchanan	Admiral, CSA	Increase Enrollment	1868-1869
Samuel Regester	Preacher	Christian Morality	1869-1873
Samuel Jones	Maj. Gen. CSA	Engineering, Mil. Training	1873-1875
William H. Parker	Navy Capt. CSA	Engineering, Mil. Training	1875-1882
Augustine J. Smith	Merchant	Increase Enrollment	1883-1887
Allen Dodge (Acting)	Banker	Find a Successor	1887-1888
Henry E. Alvord	Scientist, Major, USA	Serve the Farmer	1888-1892

The trustees' first choice for a president, two years after the Civil War ended, was Major General George Washington Custis Lee, the son of General Robert E. Lee and chief military advisor to Confederate President Jefferson Davis. The Maryland General Assembly and the press howled, and Lee graciously withdrew. The trustees turned instead to Charles L. C. Minor, a graduate of the University of Virginia, once a successful planter and a captain in the Confederate Army. Minor promised a curriculum much like Charles Calvert's, a combination of classics and science, with the hope that science would evolve into scientific agriculture. The College reopened in March 1867, with four professors and a pitiful enrollment of sixteen students; Minor arrived in the fall. Professors, available for a salary of a few hundred dollars a year, were more plentiful than southern-oriented students able to pay a few hundred dollars for tuition and board. At the end of the academic year, Minor departed.

To boost enrollment, the trustees tested again the appeal of a Confederate hero by appointing Franklin Buchanan as president. Before the war, Buchanan had served as superintendent of the Naval Academy, and during the war, he had been the highest-ranking admiral in the Confederate Navy and the South's lionized hero of the *Merrimac*. Many people in Maryland objected, but there were enough southern sympathizers who approved, and enrollment swelled to over sixty. Buchanan, however, was soon bored with his job and, like many of his predecessors, he left at the end of the year.

Next, the trustees found a Methodist preacher, Samuel Regester, whose

16. Franklin Buchanan, first superinten-dent of the United States Naval Academy, later admiral in the Confederate navy, presi-dent of the Maryland Agricultural College in 1868-1869. This photograph taken while he was president.

educational philosophy was instilling Christian morality into his youth-ful charges. Chapel services were held twice daily, and Regester person-ally taught the required course in "Revealed Religion." Country people rather liked the religious emphasis, and enrollment inched upward, al-though each year, the College's list of students carried several notations, "Ran Away."

The trustees tired of Regester and determined to move in yet another direction—to emphasize engineering, if only as a means of helping farm sons find better employment in the cities. Somehow the trustees attracted two of the ablest engineering educators anywhere. One was Samuel Jones, a graduate of West Point and a Confederate major general, who came as president. The other was William H. Parker, a graduate of the Naval Acad-emy and a Confederate navy captain, who came as professor of math-ematics and ultimately replaced Jones as president. Their courses were excellent, and, for the first time, students were coming to the College for its superior education.

Jones and Parker—theirs was really a joint administration from 1873 to 1882—were equally interested in an education, like their own, that of-fered military training. Students were "cadets" who wore Confederate-style uniforms. They marched to classes, recited their lessons at attention, ate their meals in silence, and drilled for an hour daily. Student officers wore white gloves and swords. Parker obtained the use of a naval vessel in Baltimore for summer training missions in naval tactics. He outfitted the College pond, located where McKeldin Library now stands, with model boats that engaged in mock battle. Distinguished visitors to the College were met by cannon-fire salutes.

The College was, however, Maryland's only state-supported institution of higher education, and there were plenty of reasons to be disturbed at its direction. Critics disliked its Confederate orientation, its lingering elitism, its religious orientation, its militarism. Especially they disliked its continued failure to improve the farmer's economic plight. Farm prices in the 1890s fell to an all-time low. The state's farm organizations railed against the College for its failures. From time to time, the General Assembly withheld entirely its tiny annual appropriation to the College.

The trustees tried another tack, encouraging Jones and Parker to move on, and selecting a president whose only real mission was to win friends for the embattled College. Augustine J. Smith was a Virginia gentleman of courtly manners and florid language. He transformed the militarism into a "home-like atmosphere," promising the students better food, better beds, and more amusements. No one objected to Smith's efforts, but winning

17. From the 1860s to the 1890s, the lonely and embattled little College on the hill.

friends was hardly an academic mission. After four years, Smith was exhausted. One of the trustees, Allen Dodge, took over as president, mainly with the mission of finding a successor.

Meanwhile, the Maryland General Assembly and the United States Congress were also looking for ways to appease farm discontent. In 1886, the General Assembly approved a Fertilizer Law, much like a forgotten law of a half-century before, authorizing a state official to test and approve commercial fertilizers used on farms. For lack of an office elsewhere, the official was assigned to the College. Far more than anyone realized, it was the beginning of a code of farm legislation that would center there.

More important legislation came from Congress. In 1887, President Grover Cleveland signed the bill sponsored by Congressman William Hatch of Missouri that established an agricultural experiment station in each state, which would be attached to the state's land grant college. In Maryland, as in many states, the federal appropriation of $15,000 a year for agricultural experimentation was actually more than the academic budget. More importantly, the experiment station established a new mission for the College.

Trustees of the Maryland Agricultural College fully grasped the implications of the new legislation, and immediately requested the director of their new experiment station to serve as president of the College as well. He was Henry E. Alvord, the author of four books on dairy science.

18. The President's House, completed in 1859, located where the Health Center now stands. It became a woman's dormitory in 1917 and was razed in 1962.

Almost everything about him pointed to a new era. His eight predecessors were Confederate veterans, but he was from Massachusetts and a former captain in the Union army. His was a new kind of administration—with an expense account, a secretary, a typewriter, and a telephone.

Alvord's mission for the College was equally startling—it was to be a service institution, to serve the farmer. He liked to call it a "People's College." It would serve the farmer directly, and its faculty would spend their summers visiting farm organizations to lecture on crops, breeding, and fertilizers. Almost incidentally the College would serve students as an educational institution. Alvord, with the Board's permission, eliminated tuition and room rent entirely; admission was open to almost any white male who could read. The heart of the curriculum would be horticulture, botany, and breeding. College mathematics meant field measurements, drainage, and barn construction. Chemistry meant "agricultural analyses." English meant the ability to write business letters. History meant "the privileges and duties of citizenship." Alvord increased the faculty from six to twelve, six of whom were also employees of the Experiment Station.

Everything seemed to fall into Alvord's lap. In 1890, Congress, still trying to assuage agrarian discontent, approved a Second Morrill Act, this one providing each land grant college with an appropriation of yet another $15,000 per year. The Second Morrill Act provided, for the first time in American history, that education be "without distinction of race or color." To meet this provision, the Maryland trustees provided that one-fifth of their money should be passed on to the Princess Anne Academy for African-Americans on the Eastern Shore. Still, the Maryland Agricultural College was awash in money—and consequently in popularity—as it had never been before.

The surrounding countryside was also awakening. Before 1890, the railroad stop at College Station was only a single farmhouse, owned by Charles Calvert's daughter, Ella, and a store and post office run by Calvert's son, Charles. Suddenly, however, faculty were looking for new homes. Developers began buying the land between the railroad and the campus from the Calverts; they divided the land into lots and changed the name to College Park. Alvord, always courting the public, contributed trees to the new town and helped finance a plank walkway along Calvert Road from the railroad to the campus. The town built an elementary school, located at Princeton and Hartwick roads. In 1900, developers built a streetcar line beside the railroad, and College Park was on the way to becoming a suburb.

Seeking a Mission

The old turnpike through the campus was still muddy, but the Rossborough Inn bustled with activity as headquarters of the Experiment Station and headquarters of the College farm. Around it were barns—dilapidated before Alvord's time, but now well maintained. About sixty acres were under cultivation, partly to provide food for the students, but increasingly with experimental crops. On the hill, amidst a grove of cedars and oaks, was the main building, the Barracks. In front were a parade ground, a flagpole, and a small battery of artillery pieces.

By the 1890s, there were usually about sixty men in the preparatory and freshman classes, mostly from farm families, mostly dreaming of careers in the city, but only about a dozen would remain until graduation. Tuition and housing was almost free; meals cost about $150 a year. The college uniform, with two shirts, cost about $30 more. Even Alvord retained the military system, if only as a means of keeping order. There were endless rules of behavior, including a requirement for a weekly bath. The day began with reveille at six thirty, then came breakfast and room inspection. Recitations lasted until noon, then an hour of drill, and dinner at one or two o'clock. Afternoons were for laboratory work or work on the college farm. Supper was at six, after which students were usually restricted to their rooms.

19. From 1867 to 1916, all students were cadets.

The festive event of the year, far greater than now, was a three-day commencement ceremony. Usually the governor of the state attended, along with legislative leaders, trustees, newspaper reporters, and hundreds of relatives. On Commencement Sunday, one of the state's most eminent ministers delivered a baccalaureate sermon, and the afternoon was given over to musical concerts. Monday was devoted to military drills, student orations, and dramatic productions. Finally, on Tuesday, the crowd gathered in the auditorium, which was elaborately decorated with flags and bunting, boughs and evergreens, muskets and swords. A small orchestra played; the president awarded gold and silver medals for scholarship and also for deportment. There were speeches, the awarding of degrees, and much applause. That evening, the graduates and their families had dinner at the president's house, and everyone went to a commencement ball that was the climax of all the events.

From 1867 to 1892, there were seventy-three graduates from the Maryland Agricultural College. Not many of them returned to the farm. Of the 47 whose careers can be traced, there were thirteen businessmen, seven doctors, seven lawyers, seven government workers, six engineers, three educators, two farmers, one army officer, and one clergyman.

As for the state's overall educational system of the 1890s, the free public school system was secure, available for everyone, although the tiny, ill-funded schools were often distant for farmers and African-Americans.

20. Completed in 1892, the first new building since the College opened, a gym on the first floor, and a library above

Seeking a Mission

Maryland's adult literacy rate was around 84 percent. Except for students aspiring to be doctors and lawyers, however, very few people imagined that they had much to gain from an education beyond high school.

Still, visionaries imagined colleges as the means of social progress, and the building of colleges exceeded the eagerness of students to attend. There was the Johns Hopkins University, towering above everything, a totally new kind of institution, dedicated principally to research. There was the University of Maryland in Baltimore, with its professional schools of medicine, law, dentistry, pharmacy, and nursing—all selling licenses to practice and all suffering as rival schools sprang up to offer degrees at ever cheaper rates. There were nine or ten private or religious colleges, all small and struggling, mainly teaching classics and religion, all attempting, as they said, to build character. There were four teachers' colleges run by the public schools, all doing reasonably well. There was the Baltimore Mechanic Institute and the United States Naval Academy with their highly focused missions.

Then, finally, there was the Maryland Agricultural College, still the only institution supported by both state and federal funds. The College was unusual—some would have said unfocused—in its near-free tuition, in its mix of a traditional and practical curriculum, and its mixture of education, research and public service. In this conglomerate, however, lay the way to the future.

CHAPTER V

Becoming a University, 1892-1920

The land grant colleges became, belatedly, a main source for an agricultural revolution that transformed life on the farms and in the cities as well. Benefiting from their research, Maryland's farm production doubled from 1890 to 1920, farm values tripled, and farm income quadrupled. The farmers, asserting themselves as Populists in the 1890s, regained their political voice; they won major victories in the Progressive reforms of Presidents Theodore Roosevelt and Woodrow Wilson; and they benefited from the high farm prices of World War I. Along with the agricultural revolution and farm prosperity, there were dramatic transformations of daily life—with electric lights, movies, radio, automobiles, and the first airplanes.

By discovering its mission in the world, the Maryland Agricultural College came to life—students poured in, athletics and extracurricular activities burgeoned, coeducation came, and a rah-rah spirit grew. It was this newfound purpose and newfound life that made it into a state university.

THE AGRICULTURAL AGENCIES

Almost suddenly after 1892, College Park found itself at the center of three enterprises—the Agricultural Experiment Station, the agricultural control agencies, and the Cooperative Extension Service—each one usually larger in budget than the state appropriation for the College, but all essentially managed by the College and thereby enhancing it. The Maryland Agricultural Experiment Station, with its headquarters at the Rossborough Inn, bustled with abundant funds and able scientists. It worked cooperatively with commercial suppliers, testing seeds, fertilizers, insecticides, and farm machinery. Its directors, first Henry E. Alvord, then Harry J. Patterson, won the station national recognition for new varieties

41

of tobacco and strawberries, new kinds of dairy feeds, and new kinds of control for fruit tree disease and hog disease. The Experiment Station and its associated agencies gathered research results from similar stations across the nation and flooded farmers with free bulletins on the latest discoveries— economical methods of constructing barns, the results of tests of farm machinery, the names of firms selling approved seed and supplies. Farmers loved the free service, federal funds kept growing, and the state added its contributions. By 1920, the Experiment Station and its associated agencies had an annual budget of $74,000 and were spawning branch stations throughout the state.

The agricultural control agencies based at the College included a Livestock Sanitary Service that regulated the transportation of animals into and out of the state and enforced rules of quarantine and inoculation. There was a Biological Laboratory that approved serums and insecticides and watched over slaughterhouses and veterinarians. A Dairymen's Association regulated the sale of milk products. A Board of Forestry made rules for timbering and protected state parks. Other control agencies policed the labeling of most products the farmer bought and sold and established rules for grading fruit and tobacco. By 1920, the agricultural control agencies had a combined annual budget of $49,000.

21. In 1904, Route One, as it is now called, and the Rossborough inn that became headquarters for the Agricultural Experiment Station.

Becoming a University

The Cooperative Extension Service that disseminated information to the countryside was even larger in size and implication, for it was actually reshaping rural ways of thinking. Beginning with the printed reports of the Experiment Station, the program evolved into conferences, lectures, displays, and contests. Local officials owned a railroad car that took lecturers and pamphlets into the countryside; they rented a boat to tour the Chesapeake shore. Agents organized hundreds of 4-H clubs across the state to teach young people to love the farm and to follow the advice of experts. The extension service, along with the Experiment Station, began the first summer school at College Park in 1906, designed for farmers and their wives who attended free of charge.

Extension reached its high point with the federal Smith-Lever Act of 1914, providing for a small army of demonstration agents—generally two men and one woman for each county—to visit regularly with every farmer. Maryland's program, long led by Thomas B. Symons, was one of the best anywhere. Agents taught farmers to match their crops and fertilizers to their particular soils; they taught farm wives how to bake cherry pies and how to dress their children warmly. Agents made a special effort to help African-Americans in rural areas. Princess Anne Academy for African-Americans, located on the Eastern Shore, received land grant and extension funds for courses in vocational training. By 1920, the extension service and its various programs were spending about $152,000 annually.

The Experiment Station gave the College a research mission; the control agencies gave it power; the extension program made it democratic. The College was finding its way into the American mainstream.

Riding the tide was the College's unassuming president from 1892 to 1912, Richard W. Silvester. He had grown up on a Virginia farm and stud-

22. Downtown Hyattsville, the nearest urban center, 1904.

ied agriculture at Virginia's land grant institution, and his belief in farm life was almost religious. College was for every boy who grew up on the farm. Farm children need not be concerned about admission—Silvester reestablished a prep school for those who were underprepared—and high school graduates could enter the college as sophomores or even juniors. Tuition and board was already negligible, far below costs, and students would receive 10¢ an hour for work in the Experiment Station. He liked to say that students could live at college more cheaply than at home.

In an institution so resolutely designed to please students and their parents, the professor's place was lowly. The maximum salary was $1,800 in 1912, with up to thirty-six classroom hours per week, and the faculty were usually required to spend their summers lecturing to farm groups. There was no thought of tenure or academic freedom. Teaching contracts were renewed annually, and professors were dismissed in midyear if suspected of disparaging remarks about College or State officials. In 1912, Silvester had at least eleven professors of agriculture, seven of engineering, and eight for everything else, although faculty in one field frequently taught something else.

The heart of the curriculum was agriculture—not abstract courses in botany and chemistry, but practical courses in dairying, horticulture, agronomy, field crops, and fruit trees. Engineering slowly reemerged, first called "Rural Roadbuilding" and "Farm Machinery," but evolving into civil and mechanical engineering. The engineering program produced outstanding graduates: Harry Clifton Byrd, class of 1908, who became president of the institution; Hershel Allen, class of 1910, who built the bridges over the Chesapeake Bay and Delaware River; Millard Tydings, class of 1910, who served twenty-four years in the United States Senate; and Charles M. White, class of 1913, who became president of Republic Steel Corporation. The College served the farmer by helping his sons escape the farm.

The agricultural emphasis attracted foreign students into the College, usually from the embassies in Washington. From 1900 to 1914, at least forty-five foreign students enrolled, especially from the Caribbean and South America. In later years, College Park attracted an unusual number of Asian students.

Increasingly, it was the students who gave life to the institution. Literary clubs, long dormant, came to life. The Young Men's Christian Association appeared on campus in 1900, and students began to lead the chapel devotionals. There was a glee club, a mandolin club, and at least two organizations dedicated to sponsoring dances.

The interest of College officials and students in things military waxed

23. The College in 1904: the Barracks on the left, the new Administration Building in the center, and the new Morrill Hall on the right.

24. The faculty in 1904. President Silvester is seated, fourth from the left.

and waned with the fashions of the day—at a peak under Presidents Jones and Parker and the Civil War nostalgia of the 1880s, fading under President Alvord's early-1890s Populism, reviving again with the Spanish-American War and President Theodore Roosevelt's cult of manliness. During peak periods, military drill could last for two hours a day, and the rivalry between military units became so intense that voluntary drills occupied extracurricular time. Student officers, with white gloves and gleaming swords, assumed responsibility for discipline. Militarism waned again after the College fire of 1912, reemerged in the First World War, and faded again in the 1920s.

The students' most portentous new interest, and the interest that did most to awaken the College, was athletics. At Maryland, as in most institutions, college officials had long discouraged sports as a distraction from study, a distraction from military drill and from work on the College farm. Inevitably, however, the boys competed and then formed teams, and inevitably they challenged the boys from a neighboring institution. Such activities were barely tolerated; sports records from the period hardly exist. There is a picture of a baseball team in 1887, but the College's first recorded intercollegiate game occurred in 1888, when a baseball team consisting mostly of students, plus some boys from the neighborhood, traveled to Annapolis to defeat a team from St. John's College. Two years later, a mostly College football squad lost to high school teams from Sandy Spring and Laurel.

The first officially recognized team, organized by students but approved by the College, was the 1892 football team that lost disastrously to St. John's by a score of 50-0 and then to Johns Hopkins by a score of 62-0. This was embarrassing even to President Silvester and the trustees. They appropriated $5,000 for a new building that would serve on its first floor as a gymnasium and on its second floor as a library. In 1893, the trustees employed a local farmer, H. M. Strickler, to serve as Professor of Physical Culture. Strickler conducted exercises in the gym and officially coached and played baseball and tennis; probably he coached and played on the football team as well. In 1904, the first basketball team appeared.

Silvester liked to point to new buildings as the measure of his long administration, and there were several. When he arrived, there were only three—Rossborough, the Barracks, and the president's house—plus some barns. During the 1890s, he was able to add, besides the small brick gymnasium-library, an engineering building, a chemistry engineering building, and a fine science building, later named Morrill Hall. During the next decade, he added a handsome, five-story administration building, mostly used for the agricultural agencies, and an addition to the engineering buildings.

25. The Cadet Glee Club, 1904.

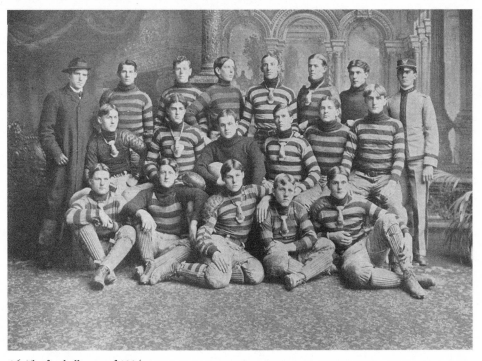

26. The football team of 1904.

The University of Maryland at College Park, A History

FIRE AND WOMEN

Then, as all seemed to be going so well, came the great fire that looked for a moment like ultimate disaster. It was November 29, 1912, the day before Thanksgiving, and the students were celebrating with a holiday ball. The auditorium of the administration building was decorated with palms and bunting, a band played, and the guests moved toward the banquet tables for the 10:30 supper. Someone shouted that the roof was on fire. Painting equipment in the attic had somehow ignited. Guests rounded up fire hoses, and the fire department from Hyattsville arrived. The wind began to rise and the water pressure to fail. Too late to save much, officials ordered the fire fighting to stop and all hands to empty the building of furniture and records. Already flames from the administration building were licking the main building that was adjacent, the five-story barracks that Calvert had built a half-century before. The Washington fire department, informed by telephone, commandeered railroad cars to send fire equipment, but no one was at the College Park station to unload it.

The two largest buildings on campus—the administration building and the Barracks— crashed into ruins. Every dormitory room was gone, many of the classrooms and offices, most of the College records. Many people assumed it was the end of the College. Silvester, brokenhearted, announced his resignation.

On the Monday after the fire, however, the faculty rallied the students on the lawn and determined to continue as usual in the remaining buildings and barns. Faculty members and nearby residents of College Park, Hyattsville, and Berwyn volunteered to rent rooms and board the students for the rest of the academic year. People from throughout the state contributed cast-off clothing for the students to wear.

The fire elevated the College into the public consciousness as never before, and the College discovered, maybe to its own surprise, that it was needed and popular. Farmers were enjoying their greatest prosperity in a century and sometimes giving the College credit for it. The public school system, now reaching into the remotest areas, was turning out graduates that increasingly wanted still more education. Governor Phillips Lee Goldsborough visited Rutgers and Cornell and returned more enthusiastic than ever about the potential of Maryland's land grant college.

The governor and the College trustees asked Harry J. Patterson, director of the Experiment Station, to take over as president. Patterson preferred research to administration, but for four years, from 1913 to 1917, he held on, and riches fell into his lap. With money from fire insurance, he quickly completed a handsome new dormitory, now Calvert Hall. Enrollments began to rise.

The greatest gains were unbidden. Student uniforms were literally gone, and students living in town enjoyed an unprecedented freedom. The military spirit, with its inspections and calisthenics, gave way to a collegiate spirit, to ideas and gaiety. Students were in charge of their own destiny as never before.

Student publications began to flourish. Students took over the faculty-controlled yearbook, *Reveille*, published since 1897, and expanded it. They took over the stuffy student newspaper, *Triangle*, changed its name to the *M.A.C. Weekly*, and bombarded the world with their opinions. In 1913, the first fraternity appeared, the group that became today's Sigma

27. The fire of 1912.

28. The ruins the next morning.

Nu. Within a year, what is now Kappa Alpha and Sigma Phi Sigma appeared; Sigma Phi Sigma was the first to have its own fraternity house. In 1920, officials recognized the first sorority, Sigma Delta.

Probably the greatest change of all was the admission of women. The federal law of 1914, providing for agricultural extension, offered the land grant colleges additional funds for home economics courses to train women as home demonstration agents. In 1916, the Maryland trustees agreed, and that fall, Elizabeth Hook and Charlotte Vaux entered as the first coeds. Patterson eventually moved into town so that the president's house could be made over into a women's dormitory. In 1917, Emma S. Jacobs received the first degree awarded to a woman, an M.A. in science; two years later, Grace B. Holmes, a transfer student, received the B.A. degree; and in 1920, Elizabeth Hook became the first four-year female graduate. By then there were more than twenty women on campus, and almost everything was different.

Even the surroundings were changing. Wilbur Wright, soon after the flights with his brother in North Carolina, arrived in College Park in 1909 to direct the United States Army in laying out the world's first graded airport. The army trained pilots there and conducted pioneering experiments. College Park was becoming a sizable village. Businesses—including a gasoline station and a lunchroom—appeared on the turnpike, now called a highway, which passed through the campus.

Farm groups, the press, and state officials generally liked the changes, probably more than the College's cautious President Patterson. In 1916, the General Assembly, with a promise of new appropriations to come, took over the College entirely, changing its name from the Maryland Agricultural College to the Maryland State College of Agriculture. The old stockholder trustees offered no protest. The new College trustees also served as a State Board of Agriculture. The new arrangement allowed Patterson to resign as president and return full-time to his research in the Experiment Station.

ALBERT F. WOODS AND THE UNIVERSITY

The new trustees were planning more expansively than at any time since the days of Charles Calvert. The trustees attracted as their new president Albert F. Woods, a noted agricultural scientist and the acting president of the University of Minnesota. For the first time, Maryland had a leader who knew first-hand what a state university was. He arrived in January 1917 with a salary of $10,000, which was nearly triple that of his

29. This famous photograph was taken at the College Park Airport in 1909, a few months after the Wright Brothers arrived there. This may be Wilbur Wright piloting the plane. The airplane outraces the train.

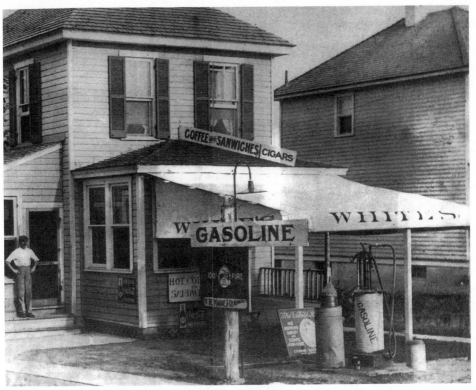

30. Bill White's Lunchroom about 1912, a College hangout, corner of College Avenue and what is now called Route One, the first commercial establishment of the present town.

predecessor and double that of the state's governor. For a while, Woods's ambitions were engulfed by the United States' entry into World War I. Students rushed off to enlist. The prep school continued, but college-level enrollment in the fall of 1917 dropped from a previous high of 201 to 140. During the next year, the government took over the land grant colleges for the all-military Student Army Training Corps. Certain army volunteers who qualified for college-level work were assigned to the institutions to continue their education under military discipline and military pay. The government rented the dormitories to serve as barracks and placed the faculty under army command. About twenty civilian students continued to attend classes, along with about 200 troops. In addition, the Army Signal Corps rented a portion of the College grounds, built temporary barracks, employed some of the faculty, and conducted a radio school for about 600 men.

As the war ended, Maryland, like most colleges, enjoyed an explosive growth. College-level enrollment rose to 246 in 1919, then to 522 in 1920. State appropriations rose accordingly, from $146,000 in 1917 to $400,000 in 1921. Profits from the army's wartime occupation allowed completion of a four-story agricultural building, now the Skinner Building.

Major Construction, 1892-1920

1893 Gymnasium and Library, two-story brick, site of Tydings Hall, cost about $5,000, razed 1958.

1894 Mechanical Engineering, two-story brick, site of west wing of Taliaferro, about $10,000, razed 1961.

1897 Chemical Building, later McDonnell Hall, three-story brick, site of Tydings, about $10,000, razed 1958. H. B. McDonnell was head of chemistry.

1898 Science Hall, later Morrill Hall, about $24,000. Justin S. Morrill was a congressman.

1904 Administration Building, five-story Gothic, southeast of Morrill Hall, about $35,000, burned 1912.

1908 Engineering, later Taliaferro, about $25,000. Thomas H. Taliaferro was Dean of Engineering.

1914 Calvert Hall Dorm, about $102,000. Charles B. Calvert was the founder.

1917 Agriculture, later Skinner Building, about $143,000. W. W. Skinner was a regent.

As the war ended, President Woods finally came into his own. With the new enrollment and prosperity, he closed down the prep school program that lingered from Silvester's day, established arts and sciences as the center of the curriculum for everyone, and then allowed students to major in special fields. He created within the College the modern system of schools, each with its own dean and budget:

School of Agriculture	Dean P. W. Zimmerman, then Dean H. J. Patterson
School of Engineering	Dean Thomas H. Taliaferro, then Dean Arthur N. Johnson
School of Arts and Sciences	Dean Thomas H. Spence, then Dean Frederick E. Lee
School of Education	Dean Harold F. Cotterman, then Dean W. S. Small
School of Home Economics	Dean Agnes Saunders, then Dean M. Marie Mount
Graduate School	Dean Charles O. Appleman

Woods was clearly moving the College toward university ranking, but the actual transformation came most pressingly from the Baltimore professional schools, where their proprietary system of selling degrees was coming to an end. Competition from rival schools caused the faculty to lower standards below where they had been a half-century before, and declining profits from student fees attracted an ever-weaker faculty. New accrediting agencies—notably the American Medical Association and the American Bar Association—threatened to withhold membership from graduates of all proprietary institutions.

Desperately the professional schools sought merger with a prosperous institution that could rescue them. They approached St. John's College in Annapolis and Western Maryland College in Westminster, but these colleges saw nothing to gain from assuming the debts from the professional schools. Clearly, the state could not do without accredited training for its doctors, lawyers, dentists, pharmacists, and nurses; clearly, the state had to come to the rescue; and clearly, the Maryland State College—the only institution of higher education owned by the state—was the reasonable partner.

Faculty from the Law School drafted the merger bill. Millard Tydings, Speaker of the House of Delegates and a graduate of both the Maryland Agricultural College and the University of Maryland Law School, introduced it. President Woods's politically astute assistant, Harry Clifton Byrd, served as chief lobbyist, and the General Assembly approved the bill unanimously. Governor Albert C. Ritchie, an archconservative, was uncomfortable with the costs that he knew were sure to come, but on April 9, 1920, he signed the merger into law. President Woods and a single Board of Regents, appointed by the governor, would assume the debts and management of the University of Maryland Schools of Medicine, Law, Dentistry, Pharmacy, and Nursing—all in Baltimore. The Maryland State College would change its name to the University of Maryland.

31. An entomology laboratory, 1899.

32. A professor's office, 1919.

33. The cadets at President Woodrow Wilson's inaugural in 1917.

34. The engineering buildings of 1920. The central building later obtained columns and became Taliaferro Hall.

The University of Maryland at College Park, A History

Despite centuries of promise from men like Edward Palmer, William Smith, John Davidge, Charles Calvert, and Libertus Van Bokkelen, a state university came slowly to Maryland. Before the merger, the state's higher education was a patchwork—Johns Hopkins University and the Naval Academy, the state-owned Maryland State College of Agriculture, four teachers' colleges run by the public school system, and a score of religious and private institutions. All received occasional pork-barrel handouts from the state, but none felt much overall responsibility for the education of the state's citizens.

Now, the new state university was much more than one of many. Now, in addition to responsibility for the state's agricultural economy, it was responsible for the state's professions, and it was also the institution mainly responsible for offering opportunity to the graduates of the state's surging high schools. These responsibilities, and others to come, would create an institution more grand than anyone imagined.

35. The coeds, 1920.

36. Flights from the College Park Airport provided many air views of the campus. This was taken in 1920.

CHAPTER VI

Jazz Age and Depression, 1920-1935

For the newly created University, the 1920s brought substantial budget increases, the 1930s brought new buildings, and in both decades, standards and enrollments rose even more. The students, however, adjusted to the changing times better than their leaders. As never before, students were in the American mainstream, expressing the country's mood in exaggerated degree—the insouciance of the Jazz Age, the resolution of the Depression. The excesses of jazz destroyed President Woods, and the cruelty of the Depression destroyed President Raymond A. Pearson, but the University flourished. College Park enrollment rose from 522 in the fall of 1920 to 1,139 when Woods left in 1926, to 2,066 when Pearson left in 1935.

The merger stimulated Woods: now he was ready to make the agricultural college worthy of its new name—a true state university—modeled not after elite institutions of the East but after the democratic state universities of the Middle West. He retained vocational and technological training, but he also built a strong liberal arts base and a graduate program; he retained outreach programs to the farm and extended such programs to the cities.

Woods went not to Governor Ritchie, who had been skeptical of the merger from the beginning, but directly to the biennial session of the General Assembly, asking that the University's 1923 budget for the Baltimore schools and College Park be increased from $443,000 a year to more than $2 million. Ritchie fought back, and the Assembly compromised with $703,000, an increase of 58 percent. At the next session, considering the budget for 1925, Woods asked for another huge increase. To Ritchie, this was impertinent and absurd. The Governor went before the General Assembly in person to call for the dissolution of the 1920 merger and the relegation of College Park back to a farmer's college. Ritchie seldom lost

59

37. Albert F. Woods, President, 1917 to 1926.

38. Adele Stamp, Dean of Women, 1922 to 1960.

his political battles, and this was the battle of the year. Newspapers and public forums took sides, essentially for and against a state university. Booming enrollment was the main argument for a university, and the General Assembly, flush with prosperity, sided with Woods. The crucial vote in the Senate was 16 to 13. The Assembly provided a budget increase of 15 percent. Once and for all, the state had decided that it had something to gain from a state university. The University's budget continued to grow, although more slowly. Ritchie, who was always adroit, began boasting of the institution as one of his finest accomplishments.

JAZZ

The students, more than administrators and politicians, established the tone of the new era. With the public egging them on, the students set out to enjoy themselves, to embrace the symbols of the decade: the pennants, raccoon coats, hip flasks, rumble seats, and floppy women's galoshes that may have added flapper to the language. The surging number of women students, called coeds, changed every aspect of student life. No longer were they oddities or demure ladies on a pedestal. They were a third of the student body; they were sometimes aggressive and their elders called them mannish. They joined the campus government association, the debate team, and the YMCA; then they created their own women's government association, women's debate team, and YWCA. There were women's teams in track, basketball, tennis, bowling, swimming, and field hockey; the women's rifle team won a national championship. In 1922, Adele Stamp arrived, the much-beloved Dean of Women for the next thirty-eight years.

Early in the decade, University authorities forbade the girls from smoking and required them to be locked in their rooms by dark each evening, but by the end of the decade the women's petitions and protests won them nearly the same privileges as men. The women had a civilizing effect on the men. The ancient rules against scuffling and racing on the stairs disappeared from the academic regulations. Gentlemanly dress became a preoccupation of the fraternities, haberdasheries became major advertisers in the student newspaper, now known as the *Diamondback*, and jacket-and-tie was standard classroom wear. About a third of the students belonged to fraternities or sororities, even with initiation fees around $150. At least two speakeasies and three lunchrooms flourished within walking distance of the campus. Nearby Bladensburg was Washington's red-light district. Student automobiles became a problem, and, in 1927, the campus police issued their first parking ticket. Faculty shared in the prosperity. The typical full professor made about $3,300 annually, lived in a large College Park house, and had a maid and an automobile.

The campus was especially lively on weekends. Dance committees assumed that every male student owned a tuxedo. The *Diamondback* in one semester counted nineteen scheduled dances in the gymnasium, four University dances in Washington hotels, plus countless hops in the fraternity-sorority houses. The most elaborate dances were in the Willard Hotel, where favors might include gold-plated penknives for men and silver pendants for women. There were house parties, boat parties, campus movies, pep rallies, picnics, teas, hayrides, and football trips. There was a college orchestra, a glee club, minstrel shows, operettas, and concerts. The College Park May Day was locally famous, attracting people from miles away to watch as suggestively costumed women acted out nursery rhymes and danced around a Maypole. Intercollegiate athletics reached a peak in the 1920s, with every student expected at every game. Football was the major sport, and Maryland became a national power. Professors dismissed classes before big games, and the University declared a holiday to celebrate the greatest victories. Coach Harry Clifton Byrd's eight-man athletic staff was far larger than most academic departments.

During the 1920s, Coach Byrd, scheduling games against the finest teams in the country, boasted 45 wins, 40 losses, and 11 ties. Students

39. Homecoming, 1924.

40. May Day, 1927.

41. The Junior Prom, 1934.

swelled with pride, and throughout the state people who otherwise knew nothing of the University learned to thrill at the exploits of its handsome coach. Byrd's teams won conference championships in football, baseball, basketball, track, and tennis; they claimed national championships in lacrosse, cross-country running, and riflery.

President Woods, however, in his earnest and self-righteous way, was never comfortable with the decade's frivolity. In the spring of 1923, when most of the girls on campus were protesting the after-dark curfew, and some were flouting their cigarettes and flirtations, Woods abruptly suspended two of the girls without quite explaining the reasons. Suddenly it was a cause celebre. Newspapers in Baltimore and Washington ran salacious stories about imagined campus activities. A professional sorority organizer, Mary Love-Collins, roared into College Park to recruit rebellious women into a chapter of Chi Omega. Some of the girls, encouraged by a newspaper reporter and by Miss Love-Collins, drew up an affidavit claiming that University administrators and faculty were seducing the co-eds. The *Washington Post* gave it front-page coverage. The story, withholding names, told of College Park "petting revels," "midnight swimming parties," and particularly of a "spanking party."

The students claimed to be outraged; the *Diamondback* employed unprecedented headlines to denounce the story; a mass meeting of students passed resolutions condemning the Chi Omega organizers, whom they blamed for the affidavit, and the *Washington Post*, which published it. Woods believed he knew who had signed the affidavit, but he was not certain. He waited until the fall term was about to begin and then sent letters to two students, Vivian Simpson and Virginia Flanagan, forbidding them to reenroll but citing merely trivial reasons, such as violating regulations by using an iron in the dormitory. Vivian Simpson sued and won readmission. The University appealed and eventually won the case against Simpson, on the grounds that an institution, meaning its president, should be able to admit students as it wished. Simpson subsequently obtained a law degree from George Washington University and was the first woman to serve as Maryland's Secretary of State.

President Woods won the case, but he was suddenly older. "I used to look forward to going to the office," he said, "but now I have headaches and look forward to going home." He remained for a year after the final court decision and then faded away into the bureaucracy of the United States Department of Agriculture.

Jazz and Depression

DEPRESSION MOOD

The lights dimmed after Woods's departure, for Raymond A. Pearson, who served from 1926 to 1935, was sour and timid. Pearson came with high credentials—New York State Commissioner of Agriculture and President of Iowa State College—but he was never able to express a goal for the University, never able to aspire to more than doing the bidding of Governor Ritchie and the Board of Regents. In his inaugural address as president, Pearson apologized for not yet knowing many people, and hoped that critics would be tolerant of his mistakes. He often contributed a column to the *Diamondback*, mainly encouraging students to study hard, attend church regularly, and not to walk on the grass. People have suggested that after his tenure in Iowa, and especially after 1929, his health was failing. In any case, people relied for decisions on his aide, Harry Clifton "Curley" Byrd.

Major Construction, 1920-1934

1920	Silvester Dorm, later Baltimore Hall, about $100,000. R. W. Silvester was a former president.
1924	Dairy Building, later Turner Hall, about $68,000. Philip C. Turner was a regent.
	Ritchie Gymnasium, later Annapolis Hall, about $163,000, razed 1988. Albert C. Ritchie was governor.
	Byrd Stadium, usually called "The Byrd Cage," seats for 5,000, site of Fraternity Row, about $100,000, razed 1952.
1928	Chemistry Building, later Silvester Hall, $210,000, razed 1971.
	Dining Hall, later LeFrak Hall, $153,000. Samuel J. LeFrak was a philanthropist.
1932	Horticulture, later Holzapfel, $138,000. Henry Holzapfel was a regent.
	Administration and Library Building, later Shoemaker, $208,000. Samuel Shoemaker was a regent.
	Women's Field House, later Preinkert, $42,000. Alma Prienkert was the University registrar.
	Ritchie Coliseum, seats for 4,200, $181,000.
	Margaret Brent Hall, later St. Mary's Hall, women's dorm, $161,000. Margaret Brent was an early settler of Maryland.
1933	Engineering Building, later part of Francis Scott Key, $99,000.

Woods sacrificed everything for faculty development, but Pearson was, if anything, a buildings president. This fit exactly with Ritchie's thinking: keep taxes and operating expenses down, but allow new construction, paid for with bonds, to encourage business during good times and recov-

42. The new gymnasium, 1924, named for Governor Albert C. Ritchie, later renamed Annapolis Hall.

43. A still newer gymnasium and coliseum of 1932, also named for Governor Albert C. Ritchie.

ery in times of recession. The initiative came from Ritchie more than Pearson: a bit more than $2 million for a Dental School building, a Law School building, and a new hospital for Baltimore; just over $1 million for new classroom buildings and dormitories at College Park.

The College Park budget for education, meanwhile, did less well, rising from $266,000 from state appropriations in 1928 to $310,000 in 1930, then crashing down to $223,000 in 1935. Departments of philosophy, classical languages, fine arts, and music died completely. Frederick E. Lee, the powerful dean of Arts and Sciences, resigned, denouncing Pearson's neglect of academic needs. In April 1933, as state revenue plunged, Ritchie and Pearson agreed that the faculty might "contribute" 10 percent of their income for the remainder of the year back to the state. For the next year, the state confirmed and increased the cut. Altogether, from 1930 to 1935, faculty salaries declined by more than 12 percent. At least twenty-four faculty with Ph.D.s departed during Pearson's administration; six were employed to take their places. The student mood changed as the Great Depression descended; ballyhoo and nonsense became immature rather than sophisticated; the students turned serious, searching, political. Pep rallies lost their spark, attendance at games declined. Curley Byrd was slowly withdrawing from coaching to devote his time to administration.

44. Byrd Stadium, 1924-1951, called "The Byrd Cage," located where Fraternity Row now stands.

45. Albert A. Pearson, the unhappy president from 1926 to 1935.

Student publications became more important; the yearbook, *Reveille*, with its military implication, became the *Terrapin*, the *Diamondback* turned its attention from dances and athletics to educational policy and politics; a literary magazine, the *Old Line*, appeared. Reactionary and radical ideas flourished. Pearson was especially concerned with what he called "the liberal problem" that seemed to radiate around the YMCA, and he expelled that organization from the campus.

As the gaiety of the 1920s exploded in the Chi Omega case, the seriousness of the 1930s culminated in even larger cases that embarrassed and weakened the institution. In 1934, Donald Murray, an African-American from Baltimore and a graduate of Amherst, applied and then sued to enter the University of Maryland Law School. Thurgood Marshall, the future Supreme Court Justice, himself once denied admission to the University's Law School, took Murray's case and won, and four years later, Donald Murray graduated from the University's Law School with distinction. The ruling applied only to the Law School, and for the next twenty years, the University usually foiled the attempts of African-Americans to register in its other professional schools. People berated the University for its integration and for its segregationist stand as well.

Meanwhile, the Ennis N. Coale case of 1933 gained even more attention. Coale, a freshman at College Park, declared himself a conscientious objector, unwilling to take the University's two-year ROTC course that was compulsory for male students. Pearson suspended him. The issue, in its largest implication, was compulsory military training in the land grant colleges. The American Association of Universities and the Methodist Church of the United States rallied behind Coale; the American Legion and the *New York Times* supported Pearson. A Baltimore court ruled for Coale, the Court of Appeals ruled for Pearson, and the United States Supreme Court allowed the Pearson victory to stand. At best it was a Pyrrhic victory, for the University was standing for militarism and compulsion.

Pearson's days were clearly numbered. Whether the troubles were his fault or not, people yearned for a new deal. The *Diamondback* in 1935, with a brilliant and daring editor, J. Marshall Mathias, began a drumbeat of criticism of the administration. More faculty resignations came, generally blaming Pearson for neglect of things academic. The alienated former dean, Frederick E. Lee, now at the University of Illinois and eager to return as Pearson's replacement, fed information to Pearson's critics. The Board of Regents sent questionnaires to the faculty, asking for their anonymous evaluation of the president, and forty-eight of the fifty-four replies expressed a desire for change. The regents gave Pearson four days, until July 1, 1935, to resign. Pearson's smiling assistant, Curley Byrd, was in command.

46. Harvesting hay in the 1930s along Route One, near North Gate.

CHAPTER VII

The Age of Curley Byrd, 1935-1954

Harry Clifton Byrd—everyone except the faculty called him Curley—did more for the University than anyone in its history. For almost fifty years—from 1905 when he arrived as an all-sports athlete until his departure in 1954 to run for governor—he was usually the largest presence on campus and often seemed to be dictating its direction. His free-wheeling manner attracted plenty of controversy, but during his nineteen years as president, from 1935 to 1954, College Park enrollment rose from 2,000 to 9,000; the annual state appropriation rose from $1.5 million to $9.8 million; and the plant value rose from $3 million to $37 million.

Much of his power lay in his appearance and charisma. "The Devil Hath Power to Assume a Pleasing Shape" said the college yearbook beneath his graduation picture. Sometimes, said the yearbook, when a large number of boys went into town, they bribed Curley to go along in order to be assured of attracting enough girls for all of them. Many years later, when he was mentioned as a possible candidate for president of the United States, a columnist called him "the handsomest man in American politics." Divorced the year before he became the University's president, he gaily escorted college coeds to dances, and he delighted in making light insinuations about his amours in his public speeches. He was warm, generous, egalitarian, always ready to reach into his pocket for five dollars or more for a student in need or a campus janitor.

His leading critics were the Sunpapers editors of Baltimore, unfriendly to most public support for higher education and regularly furious at Byrd's success with the General Assembly. Sunpapers reporters, however, notably H. L. Mencken, regularly fell under Byrd's spell. Mencken, to torment his editors, celebrated Byrd's flamboyance, and suggested that Johns Hopkins University might well humble itself to become part of Byrd's empire. Byrd's other critics were faculty members. They were suspicious

71

47. Harry Clifton "Curley" Byrd, the happy president from 1935 to 1954.

of a football coach as their president, ruffled by his non-intellectualism, offended by his disdain of faculty government. Too obviously he preferred the company of students or politicians to that of professors.

Curley grew up in Crisfield, on the Eastern Shore, and remained in high school an extra year to play ball. He arrived at the Maryland Agricultural College as a sophomore, and was soon quarterback and captain of the football team, pitcher for the baseball team, star of the track team, and the campus tennis champion. Records of the early basketball games are vague, but surely he was there. He graduated in engineering in 1908, and for the next three years played for whatever school would make it worth his while. Such play by students taking a graduate course was more or less legal then. One year he played for Georgetown and put that institution on the sports map, and the next year he ran track for Western Maryland and won that school a state championship. In the spring of each year, he played professional baseball for Cambridge and then for San Francisco. For a while, he was a sports writer for *The Washington Star*.

Four years after he graduated, he was back in College Park as instructor of English and coach of football, baseball, basketball, track, tennis, and lacrosse. He was better as a coach than as an English instructor. During his twenty-two years as football coach, from 1912 to 1934, he scheduled the best teams within traveling distance, winning 117 games, losing 82, and tying 15. He was ready to move into a larger realm.

Three successive presidents—Patterson, Woods, and Pearson—called him in as their assistant. He provided vision and enthusiasm. He was their diplomat to the world—to the students, alumni, newspaper reporters, members of the General Assembly, and especially to the Governor. Curley, for his part, was discovering that politics was more fun than winning games, that he could build a university worthy of his teams.

After the Baltimore-College Park merger that he helped engineer, the professional schools knew they reported not only to Woods and Pearson, but also to the president's assistant. He was also the unofficial dean of men. He gave the *Diamondback* its name, selected the terrapin as the school's mascot and is said to have provided its name, Testudo. The Alumni Association petitioned that the new 1923 football stadium, located where Fraternity Row now stands, be named "Curlie Byrd Stadium."

THE NEW DEAL

Almost from the moment Byrd took over as president in 1935, his luck and maneuvering paid off. As though a dam had burst, money was suddenly plentiful. A classmate and friend, Charles E. McManus, provided College Park with an endowment of $150,000, and a Baltimore physician, Frank C. Bressler, provided the medical school with nearly $1 million. Byrd cultivated the friendship of the rising aircraft manufacturer, Glenn L. Martin, who began by offering small gifts to the College Park engineering program and eventually gave almost $5 million.

The New Deal was hitting its stride in Washington, and Byrd did not merely wait for his share. He was everywhere, wheedling, demanding. He gathered in $100,000 a year for new programs in agricultural education, he made the University a regional headquarters for training instructors in the Civilian Conservation Corps, and he obtained from the National Youth Administration some $40,000 a year that paid students for part-time work in the libraries, laboratories, dining hall, or as clerical help for professors.

Byrd, who had been a political conservative in the 1920s, wrote a sparkling defense of the New Deal programs, invited Mrs. Eleanor Roosevelt to speak on campus, received invitations to the White House, and collected nearly $3 million in Works Progress Administration construction funds, one of the largest amounts given to any university. President Roosevelt, however, drove a hard bargain: Byrd was forced to join Roosevelt's effort in 1938 to defeat the reelection to the United States Senate of Maryland's conservative Democrat, Millard E. Tydings. This was painful, for Byrd and Tydings had been classmates and were friends. The Tydings purge failed; Byrd and Tydings made up; and soon, the two of them were working together again to obtain more federal money for the University. Lobbying together in Washington, they outmaneuvered Colorado in making College Park a research headquarters for the United States Bureau of Mines, and they beat out Massachusetts in making it a headquarters for fisheries and wildlife research.

Byrd's greatest sorcery came with the Governor and General Assembly. Just as he was switching from conservative to liberal to court President Roosevelt, he was transferring his allegiance from Democratic Governor Ritchie to the new Republican Governor Harry Nice. Partly with Nice's support, partly with farm support mobilized by his agricultural agents, and partly by the charm of his personal lobbying, the state's 1937 appropriation for the University rose by an incredible 85 percent, with another million dollars for construction. The Baltimore Sunpapers raged in vain.

Byrd loved construction projects, and his new buildings, plus his sense of style, changed the face of the campus, shifting its center from in front of Morrill Hall to the present-day McKeldin Mall. Byrd employed the Olmsted Brothers of Boston—descendants of Frederick Law Olmsted—for landscape advice. He closed University Boulevard, then called University Lane, that then extended eastward through the campus, and rerouted it north of the campus. He imposed a uniform neo-Georgian style of brick facades, white columns, broad steps to the second floor of his buildings, and fine cupolas when he could afford them. From his days as assistant president he presided over the construction of St. Mary's, Ritchie Coliseum, Shoemaker, and Holzapfel (1932). Then, during his first years as president, came Anne Arundel dormitory and H. J. Patterson Hall (1937), Francis Scott Key (1938), what is now Microbiology (1939), Symons, Marie Mount, the Administration Building, the Armory and five more dormitories (1940).

Major Construction, 1935-1954

1937   H. J. Patterson Hall, originally used for Arts and Sciences, $284,000. H. J. Patterson was a former president.

Anne Arundel Dorm, $189,000.

1938   Engineering Building, later Francis Scott Key, $212,000.

1939   Bureau of Mines Building, later Microbiology, acquired by University in 1938, $350,000.

1940   Main Administration, $225,000.

Rossborough Inn, completed in 1804, remodeled, $70,000.

Washington and Howard Dorms, $175,000.

Poultry and Agriculture, later Symons Hall, $194,000. Thomas B. Symons was dean of agriculture.

Home Economics, later Marie Mount, $204,000. Marie Mount was dean of home economics.

Armory, said to be bomb-proof, later Reckord Armory, $449,000. Milton A. Reckord was a general.

Harford, Prince George's, Kent Dorms, $413,000.

1947   Thirty-three temporary buildings, about $1,200,000, razed over following thirty years.

1948   Symons Hall addition, $348,000.

Classroom Building for College of Education, later Woods Hall, $283,000. Albert F. Woods was a former president.

1949   Glenn L. Martin Engineering Building, $1,200,000. Glenn L. Martin was a philanthropist.

Engineering Laboratories, $974,000.

Chemical Engineering, $583,000.

Wind Tunnel, $1,241,000.

Somerset, Queen Anne Dorms, $846,000.

1950   423 acres, College Park, $370,000

1951   Chemistry Building, $1,780,000.

Byrd Stadium, originally seats for 35,000, $618,000.

1952   Physics Building, later John S. Toll Physics Building, $995,000. John S. Toll was head of physics and chancellor of the University System.

Memorial Chapel, $627,000.

1953   Mathematics Building, $750,000.

Fraternity Row, 10 houses, $890,000.

Student Union, later Adele Stamp Student Union, $710,000. Adele Stamp was dean of women.

Industrial Education, later J. M. Patterson, $312,000. J. M. Patterson was a regent.

1954   Allegany, Charles, Montgomery, Caroline, Carroll, Wicomico Dorms, $2,194,000.

The University of Maryland at College Park, A History

As important as the newfound prosperity were the educational changes of the 1930s—changes promoted by educational philosophers like John Dewey, changes that the times required. The new educational philosophy called for fewer recitations, for courses that were relevant to the issues of the day, and for more use of libraries and laboratories.

The College of Arts and Sciences remained the center of the College Park curriculum, receiving most of the funds from the first budget increases. Everyone agreed, at least for the moment, that libraries and laboratories needed the greatest boost. In the revised curriculum, English and language classes emphasized social criticism. Historians discovered that their truths changed with each generation and that their own generation needed to explore politics, economic change, and ideology. Mathematics and sciences, where the old absolutes first began to crumble, emphasized probabilities and relativity. The fine arts and music revived, mainly as subjects for aspiring teachers in the public schools.

A College of Business and Public Administration emerged. In the 1920s a school of business had appeared and died; in 1938 a College of Commerce emerged, and four years later it changed its name and broadened its purview to incorporate the booming fields of economics and government. Economists discovered John Maynard Keynes and studied comparative economic systems. Government professors studied parties, pressure

48. Francis Scott Key Hall, central and western sections completed in 1938; originally for engineering, later for arts and humanities.

groups, and ideology.

The Colleges of Education and Home Economics prospered; Colleges of Agriculture and Engineering held their own and added especially to their extension work. In Baltimore, the medical school added courses in public health and turned from theory to clinics, diagnosis, and treatment. The Law School gave new emphasis to case study and added a legal aid clinic.

Byrd abolished salary scales in order to pay his best professors whatever the market demanded. Annual salaries for full professors varied from $1,800 to $5,900. Generally this was a progressive step, except that Byrd alone approved all salaries, and the president's critics learned to hold their tongue. Full-time College Park faculty increased from 137 in 1935, of whom 37 percent had Ph.D.s, to 212 in 1941, of whom 59 percent had Ph.D.s.

By 1940, the smell of war was spreading over the campus. The ROTC staff expanded, and "Military Day," replete with mock battles, became a spring festival. After Pearl Harbor, the campus went on a three-semester, year-round basis. Students were admitted with less than a high school diploma, and some graduated in slightly more than two years. The ROTC, presumably for training purposes, posted a 24-hour guard around the administration building. An officer-training program, the Army Specialized Training Program, brought 1,400 men to campus, took over most of the dormitories for military barracks, and marched the men to classes with what remained of the civilian students.

POSTWAR MOOD

The student mood was ever changing. Long gone was the happy ballyhoo of the 1920s, along with the resolution and school loyalty of the 1930s. The early 1940s was distinctive for its wartime dislocation, and during Byrd's last years as president, from the late 1940s until 1954, there was student crowding and a growing peevishness that almost overshadowed Byrd's continuing triumphs. The institution that for so long begged for students was suddenly overwhelmed—from 4,200 students at College Park in the fall of 1945 to 8,600 just one year later. After that, the numbers leveled off for a decade. All white high school graduates were eligible for admission, plus almost any white student over the age of 21. The sudden doubling of admissions from 1945 to 1946 came from a four-year wartime backlog of students, from the G.I. Bill that provided free tuition for veterans, and from postwar prosperity. The crunch came in most American colleges, but especially at College Park. For a while, 700 men

49. The new Administration Building, completed in 1940, was guarded round the clock by cadets when the war began.

50. A view of the campus about 1942.

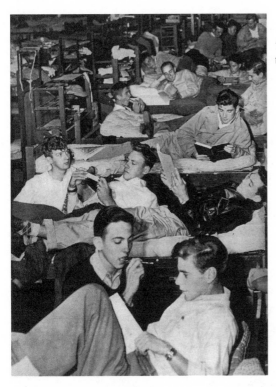

51. In September, 1946, 700 men camped in the Armory, sleeping in double-decker bunks.

52. The University acquired 33 temporary barracks for veteran housing and for classrooms.

camped in double-decker bunks in the armory, and women students lived four to a room. From seven o'clock in the morning until six at night, Saturdays included, students rushed into classes in hopes of finding a seat. Sometimes lines in the dining hall lasted an hour. While Byrd exhorted the legislature for building funds, he purchased from the army scores of temporary wooden structures that appeared haphazardly over the campus.

Before the war, most of the students had lived on campus, but now most were veterans and commuters who lived in surrounding communities. Five hundred veteran student families lived in surplus housing across the campus or beyond, as far away as Greenbelt.

The postwar students had their distinctive look, a combination of conformity and rebellion. Most men wore crew cuts; fraternity men sported loud ties and checkered sports jackets; the vets often wore army fatigues. Women wore long hair, bobby socks, and saddle oxfords.

While students blamed their once-beloved president for campus shortcomings, the faculty had never felt close to him. Faculty salaries lagged behind inflation. Faculty income in the early 1950s was probably lower, relative to income in other professions, than at any other time in the institution's history.

Campus discontent only drove Byrd deeper into politics. He was generous with free scholarships for each member of the General Assembly to give to family or friends, and generous with the use of alumni and farm extension mailing lists for the candidates he approved. State appropriations to College Park rose from $1.3 million in 1945 to $4.1 million in

53. Endless lines—for the dining hall, or for seats in a classroom, 1946.

54. The campus in 1949. University Boulevard, then called University Lane, extends through the campus to join Route One near Ritchie Coliseum.

1948, to $9.7 million in 1954. At least $9 million came for new construction. Byrd succeeded as well for the professional schools in Baltimore. The Veterans Administration believed Byrd collected from them $2.3 million more than was due, but the agency never recovered the money.

POSTWAR DIRECTIONS

Byrd no longer aspired for mere popularity, or even for status as a state university, but for renown. His main trait, besides his charm and cunning, was his ambition. His postwar initiatives were as daring as ever, often successful, and often controversial.

The most successful was the expansion of off-campus classes into what was for a while the largest adult education program in the world. Now it exists apart from College Park as University College. At first, the program offered night classes to working people in nearby urban centers in the state, then to nearby army bases. The armed services were delighted to have their officers and enlisted men pursuing academic degrees, and soon the Army and Air Force were paying most of the costs. Maryland obtained almost exclusive access to the troops, and classes spread to overseas bases. By 1954, about 150 faculty were teaching each year approximately

55. Glenn L. Martin helped the University construct its new science and engineering buildings.

56. Physics left, Mathematics center, Chemistry behind.

57. Memorial Chapel, a new symbol for the campus.

10,000 armed forces students outside of the United States; by 1964, there were 450 faculty and 40,000 military students overseas. Commanders on some bases established continuing education as an unwritten requirement for promotion. Many students obtained degrees from the University of Maryland, and many transferred their credits to other institutions. Some of the faculty teaching on overseas bases were on leave from the College Park campus, and volunteering for these assignments was a valued perk; other faculty were employed especially for overseas service. Accreditation agencies ranked standards in off-campus courses to be at least equal to those of the home campus.

Another Byrd initiative, the "American Civilization" program, was more controversial than successful. Byrd attempted to break down disciplinary lines and give focus to education by requiring all students to devote their first two years to the study of American history, American government, American literature, and American sociology, combined for men with ROTC military service. The program gained national attention. The *New York Times* and the Hearst newspapers delighted in the program, but many faculty considered it chauvinistic, and gradually it faded away.

Equally controversial was Byrd's haste to solve what he called "the race problem" by pouring money into Princess Anne Academy, which he renamed Maryland State College, the University's distantly related branch for African-Americans located on the Eastern Shore. Byrd liked to think of himself as promoting African-American education, but another intent was to blunt African-American demands for integration at College Park.

The ruse failed, for the courts were pressing. In 1951, fearing or yielding to court action, the University admitted Hiram Whittle as the first African-American undergraduate at College Park, and in 1952, Parren Mitchell completed all of his classes on campus and received an M.A. degree in sociology. Finally, in 1954 came the Supreme Court's decision in *Brown v. Board of Education*. The decision allowed a year of delay, but the regents ordered immediate compliance, and that fall, African-Americans were admitted, almost without notice. Byrd, in his search for solutions, had merely entangled himself and was soon to be attacked both for segregation and for integration.

Then there was Byrd's enthusiasm for athletics. That enthusiasm had waned in the 1930s, perhaps as a matter of tactics, but it roared back after the war. In 1950, Byrd created a College of Physical Education, Recreation, and Health—replete with thirty-four faculty members, nearly 100 courses, and a Ph.D. program. Byrd also found the football coach he wanted, Jim Tatum from Oklahoma. Tatum was one of the best coaches in the country, and Byrd provided him with an abundance of scholarships to distribute, superb facilities, and no questions about his players' academic performance.

58. The Alpha Chi Omega sorority sisters, 1953. They liked saddle oxfords.

The Age of Curley Byrd

The victories poured in—invitations to the Gator Bowl in 1947 and 1949, the Sugar Bowl in 1951, the Orange Bowl in 1953 and 1955. In 1953, Maryland ranked as college football's national champion. Byrd liked for Maryland to be in the headlines. Students at College Park were pleased with victories, of course, but the proportion of students attending games lagged far behind the golden days when Curley was the quarterback and coach.

Byrd's ambition pressed on. By 1954, almost everyone took for granted that Byrd was the strongest man, if not the boss, of the state's Democratic Party; that if he wanted to be the state's governor, his nomination was a certainty; and that his election over the Republican incumbent, Theodore McKeldin, was an overwhelming probability. Byrd resigned as president to devote full time to the campaign. Then, at the last moment, a wealthy spoiler, Baltimore contractor George P. Mahoney, crashed into the Democratic primary, attacking Byrd as an academic liberal who tolerated student excesses and allowed integration at College Park. Byrd barely squeaked by, only to face the eloquent McKeldin in the general election. McKeldin attacked him as a conservative, an authoritarian administrator, and a racist who had resisted integration. Most important, said McKeldin, Byrd's University of Maryland, so much acclaimed, was in danger of losing its accreditation.

The accreditation charge was true. The Middle States Association of Colleges and Secondary Schools had just completed its review, undertaken each decade, and the report that Byrd had anticipated as a crown on his career was in fact a disaster. The Baltimore medical school was below standards, according to the report; at College Park, athletics were overwhelming everything, the library was a disgrace, and faculty government hardly existed. The University would lose its accreditation unless changes came immediately.

McKeldin was elected governor and joined with the Board of Regents in procuring a new University president; then he happily supported the new president's effort to raise academic standards up to the level of the University's prosperity and acclaim. Beyond the campus, President Dwight Eisenhower was promising prosperity and calling for consensus. For College Park, there was a new direction.

59. From 1953 to 1955, Jim Tatum's football teams were contenders for the national championship.

60. A pep rally, 1953.

CHAPTER VIII

Quality and Quantity, 1954-1970

From 1954, when Wilson H. Elkins, a Rhodes Scholar, became presi-dent, until about 1970, the themes that dominated the College Park story were rising academic standards and soaring enrollment. An Elkins convo-cation address was entitled "A Quantity of Quality." At first, the two goals were complementary, but standards and numbers also brought ten-sions. The campus, as usual, reflected the world beyond. Eisenhower pros-perity and the ideal of consensus in the 1950s gave way, in the early 1960s, to the idealism of Presidents John F. Kennedy and Lyndon Johnson and, later in the decade, to disillusionment and anger that came with the war in Vietnam. By 1970, the campus was writhing in turmoil.

Rising standards and skyrocketing expansion was the story of higher education throughout the country. Enjoying a post-war prosperity, the United States created the National Science Foundation, vastly expanded the National Institutes of Health, and, after Russia's Sputnik, enacted the National Defense Education Act (1958), all of which poured money into the universities. National college enrollments more than tripled from 1954 to 1970; College Park enrollment grew by 380 percent.

THE CLIMATE OF LEARNING

For eight months in 1954, while Byrd was running for governor and while the regents were recruiting a new University president, Thomas B. Symons served as acting president. A quiet, comfortable man, a longtime professor and dean of agriculture, Symons possessed no imperial ambi-tion, merely the desire to please his faculty colleagues, although that was something no one had done in a long time. He transformed the remodeled Rossborough Inn into a faculty club that was quickly vibrant with faculty life and faculty ideas. During the torrid governor's race, he bound the

61. Wilson H. Elkins, the spokesman for quality, President from 1954 to 1970.

University's agricultural agents to unaccustomed political neutrality.

The regents, meanwhile, selected for the institution's permanent president the soft-spoken Texan, Wilson H. Elkins. He, like Byrd, was a noted athlete. At the University of Texas in the late 1920s, he was famous as "Bull" Elkins, captain of the basketball team and quarterback of the football team that won the Southwest Conference title. He was president of the student body and graduated Phi Beta Kappa. He learned in college a habit that stuck with him, getting up at 4:00 a.m. to study. On his Rhodes Scholarship to Oxford University in England, he wrote a doctoral dissertation on British-American trade relations. For two years, he taught history at the University of Texas, for ten years, he was president of a junior college in Texas; then for six years, he served as president of what is now the University of Texas, El Paso.

Quality and Quantity

His personality reflected the new mood in higher education—quiet, cautious, moderate. He was formal rather than familiar; no one called him anything but "Dr. Elkins." He was direct rather than cunning; his statements were always qualified but never evasive; and he was bull-like determined. He believed in opportunity—he was the first in his family to attend college—but with opportunity came self-discipline, high standards, and achievement.

Students also were changing, becoming more serious and purposeful. Probably the main reason for this change was the growing necessity for an academic degree to obtain a job. The campus had become a training ground for life; the college transcript and whatever grades it carried was as essential for employment as a clean shirt had been in earlier generations. Major corporations had personnel recruiters on campus each spring, and the once-gentlemanly grades of C had become marks of mediocrity. Other reasons for the changed attitude lay in the growing pressure for admission to college, the rising proportion of graduate students, and the uncertainty of life in a world with a mushroom cloud. "Academic performance," said Elkins, "is becoming socially acceptable."

Extracurricular activities continued, of course—the fraternities and sororities, the athletics, the dances—but they were more self-conscious, part of the cultivation of the well-rounded life that job recruiters valued. Students cultivated moderation; fraternities and sororities played down pranks and snobbery and encouraged social responsibility; dormitory and commuter groups became almost like fraternities. Other student activities gained in importance—student government, student publications, drama groups, professional clubs, and honoraries. The humor magazine, *Old Line*, faded way, and the literary magazines, *Expression* and the *Calvert Review* flourished. The *Diamondback* emphasized academic affairs and world events, almost ended its coverage of dances and social affairs, and relegated sports to the back pages. *Maryland*, the alumni magazine, shortened its accounts of reunion banquets to make room for serious articles, sometimes by the faculty, on issues of the day.

The saddle oxfords and army fatigues of the early 1950s gave way to the Ivy League look—short hair, subdued colors, and a tailored look for women; penny loafers, khaki trousers, button-down blue shirts for men, along with a gray flannel suit and a challis tie for special occasions.

The happy and conformist student spirit was also reflected in warming public support for higher education. Russia's Sputnik had preceded American satellites into space, and people worried about mediocrity. Words like "intellectual" and even "egghead" began to assume a favorable connotation. Governor McKeldin boasted of his love for the University, and the Baltimore Sunpapers warmed to Elkins' talk of excellence. The General Assembly, no longer suspicious of University requests, began working with the institution, sometimes even adding items to its budget. From 1954 to 1970, the state appropriation for College Park rose from $9.8 million to $35.6 million; the value of its physical plant increased from $37 million to $159 million.

The pleasant climate for higher education brought benefits from beyond the state. The National Defense Education Act of 1958 provided direct federal appropriations for science and languages, plus loans for students. Foundations like Ford, Carnegie, and Rockefeller gave increasingly large sums to academic programs. Most importantly, government and industry turned more and more to the universities for research, paying the salaries of research professors and graduate students to investigate particular problems. University research grants rose from $2.5 million in 1954, mostly in agriculture, to $32.7 million in 1970, mostly in the physical and health sciences.

INGREDIENTS OF QUALITY

Within two weeks of his arrival, President Elkins called the first general faculty meeting that had occurred in decades, and he asked the faculty to take the initiative in organizing an assembly to share in campus gover-

62. McKeldin Library, named for the man who defeated Curley Byrd in the race for governor.

nance. A committee drafted a plan that Elkins and the regents approved, creating a faculty senate, presided over by the president and including twenty-seven ex-officio administrators and sixty-eight elected faculty members. The Senate soon had twenty-one standing committees that dealt with every aspect of University life. The whole University, and, eventually, each campus of the University had faculty assemblies that could refer matters to the Senate. For a while, everyone delighted in the new government. "The voice of the faculty is heard again in the land of the terrapin," said Elkins.

Elkins expanded his administrative staff, and the faculty saw the expansion not as bureaucracy but as evolution away from the one-man rule that had long prevailed. Albin O. Kuhn, from the College of Agriculture, became Vice President in charge of financial and physical plant affairs. R. Lee Hornbake, from the College of Education, became Vice President for Academic Affairs. There was a new dean for student affairs and new directors for development and public relations.

Faculty salaries began to rise, by 20 percent after Elkins's first budget went into effect, by more than 200 percent by 1970. Inflation was rising too, but faculty salaries were finally closing the gap with other occupations. Faculty gained Social Security coverage in 1956, and retirement benefits increased. By 1970, the average ten-month salary for full professors was $22,500, and some were earning twice as much.

The Faculty Senate adopted a tenure policy, accepted by Elkins and the regents, assuring academic freedom and job security to faculty, usually after about six years of service. Academic freedom was a new concept at College Park. The Senate also adopted a sabbatical policy—heretofore at the whim of the president—that allowed productive faculty at least a half-year in every seven years for full-time research. A patent policy allowed faculty a portion of the returns from their research. Professors gained a major voice in determining promotions and teaching schedules; they gained almost full control over classroom procedures and examinations. These were big steps in the 1950s.

One of the greatest boosts to faculty morale came in 1956 with the creation of the Senate's General Research Board, which provided summer salaries and equipment for faculty engaged in promising research. The grants especially benefited faculty in the humanities, who did not share proportionately in government research contracts. By 1970, the Board was awarding about seventy grants annually.

At least as important as improving the faculty was raising standards for the students. The Faculty Senate adopted an Academic Probation Plan that went into effect in 1957. It provided that if a student's average fell below C, or if a student failed to make junior standing after five semesters, then he or she was placed on academic probation under special supervision. If the student failed to better his or her standing after one semester on probation, he or she was dismissed. Falling on generations of academic deadwood, almost 14 percent of the students were dismissed during the first year. A few parents and students howled, but generally the public approved. The dismissals gave the University a reputation for quality that pleased the General Assembly, and pleased most parents as well.

For the first time in its history, the University began rejecting some high school graduates for admission. High school graduates with less than a C average were required to attend the University's Summer School, and their fall admission depended on good grades in specified courses. The proportion of entering freshmen who had graduated in the top 10 percent of their high school class rose from 12 percent in 1954 to 21.6 percent in 1970. The faculty increased the number of basic required courses from eight to twelve, with additional work in mathematics, science, and social science. The requirement in physical education dropped from two years to one. While eliminating weak students, the faculty also launched an hon-

63. The Rossborough Inn, built in 1804, a farm building after about 1835, rebuilt as headquarters for the Experiment Station in 1888, restored to near original form in 1940, and used mostly as a faculty club after 1954.

ors program to provide extra stimulation for students who were outstanding. Most departments provided special sections where honors students worked with the best teachers. In their junior and senior years, the students did special research in their field, took an oral exam, and graduated with "honors" or "high honors." The program offered scholarships and provided students with superior lodging. Some departments, such as mathematics, actively recruited honors students from the high schools.

Chairs of the University Senate

From 1954 to 1970, the Senate, with membership from all campuses, usually included 68 faculty and 27 administrators. From 1971 to the present, the Senate, with all members from College Park, usually included 68 faculty, 20 staff, 20 undergraduates, 17 deans, and 9 graduate students.

1955-1970	Wilson H. Elkins	The President
1971-72	Melvin Bernstein	Music
1972-73	David Falk	Physics
1973-74	Neill Singer	Economics
1974-75	Jacob Goldhaber	Mathematics
1975-77	Don Piper	Government and Politics
1977-79	Shirley S. Kenny	English
1979-80	Jacob Goldhaber	Mathematics
1980-82	Howard Brinkley	Zoology
1982-84	Betty Smith	Textiles
1984-85	L. John Martin	Journalism
1985-86	Ralph Bennett	Architecture
1986-87	Janet Hunt	Sociology
1987-88	Andrew Wolvin	Speech
1988-89	Richard Farrell	History
1989-90	Don Piper	Government and Politics
1990-91	Bruce Fretz	Psychology
1991-92	Gerald Ray Miller	Chemistry
1992-93	Robert Lissitz	Education
1993-94	Hank Dobin	English
1994-95	Christopher Davis	Electrical Engineering
1995-96	Charles Wellford	Criminal Justice
1996-97	John D. Anderson	Aerospace Engineering
1997-98	Marvin Breslow	History
1998-99	Denny Gulick	Mathematics
1999-00	William B. Walters	Chemistry
2000-01	Mark P. Leone	Anthropology
2001-02	Ellie Weingaertner	Staff, Graduate School
2002-03	Kent Cartwright	English
2003-04	Joel Cohen	Mathematics
2004-05	Arthur Popper	Biology

Teaching methods changed during Elkins's administration; new fields of study appeared, some fields declined. Everyone kept repeating that good teaching was important; the regents created a number of $1,000 awards for faculty who excelled as teachers; and the departments kept experimenting with new ways to reach the students. Departments like history and economics used their regular faculty for lecture sections for up to 300 students and allowed graduate assistants to meet once a week with small sections of about twenty. Mathematics, sociology, and zoology transferred basic courses to television. Foreign languages used electronic teaching machines. All this was modernization; incidentally, the changes usually allowed the faculty more time for research.

The best department during Elkins's administration was physics, an excellence that was mainly the creation of its dynamic chairman, John S. Toll. On many nights, Toll never left his office and labs, napping on a couch. With federal money, his department built a cyclotron for the study of nuclear particles, and it added work in astronomy and in cosmic ray, high energy, molecular, and plasma physics. A computer science program began early, in 1962, and emerged as one of the strongest in the country. Economics, under Dudley Dillard, gained national visibility. Other departments believed they were outstanding.

64. Heidleberg, Germany, was the European headquarters of the University's overseas program. In the 1950s and 1960s, it was the largest American extension program in the world.

Quality and Quantity

The College of Arts and Sciences added work in several branches of mathematics and in anthropology, classics, philosophy, music, and the arts. Engineering expanded its work in aeronautical, chemical, and civil engineering. New colleges of library science and architecture emerged.

The two declining programs of the Elkins years were ROTC and athletics. The ROTC requirement for male students was relaxed, first for conscientious objectors, then for transfer students. In 1963, the requirement dropped from two years to one, and after 1965, ROTC courses were no longer compulsory.

Jim Tatum, Byrd's great football coach, understood the meaning of rising academic standards and, in 1956, announced his departure. Still there were moments of glory. In 1957, England's Queen Elizabeth II attended a Maryland football game; Maryland won, and the press worldwide hailed it as a grand moment of American sports. One year later, Maryland opened an eighteen-hole golf course, paid for from the profits from past bowl games. In other sports, there were conference championships. No longer, however, was Maryland mainly an athletic kingdom. The number of athletic scholarships declined; the graduation rate of athletes increased. From 1955 to 1970, the football team

65. The Queen's Game, October, 1957. Left to right: Coach Tommy Mont (in front of President Elkins), Queen Elizabeth II, Governor Theodore McKeldin, Prince Philip.

66. Fraternity Row, 1955.

had six different coaches, and together they produced 68 wins and 92 losses. The College of Physical Education shrank.

An early capstone to Elkins's quest for quality came in 1964 with the establishment of a Maryland chapter of Phi Beta Kappa. It was, of course, the country's oldest and most famous scholarship society, serving the academic world almost as a super-accreditation agency, accepting as members only those institutions judged to have the soundest academic programs. Twice before, in 1925 and 1948, Maryland had been rejected for membership. Now, ten years after Elkins's arrival, the campus basked in academic approval. The *Washington Post* gave it a headline, "The Brains At Maryland Are Beginning to Show." In 1969, the American Association of Universities accepted Maryland into membership, thus ranking it among the top fifty research institutions in the nation.

THE EDUCATION EXPLOSION

By the mid-1960s, the University's growing quality was giving way to concern with its overwhelming size. For his first ten years as president, Elkins basked in acclaim for the clear direction he provided; for the next ten years or so, he was responding, first to swelling numbers, then to swelling discontent. The more standards rose, the more people wanted to attend. Enrollment rose steadily after 1954 and contributed to the University's strength, but, during the 1960s, the increase reached landslide proportions that altered the temper and structure of the institution. Enrollment rose from approximately 9,000 in 1954 to 14,000 in 1960, to 26,000 in 1965, and to 35,000 in 1970. There the University capped enrollment, but, by then, College Park was an educational colossus, the third or maybe just the seventh largest campus in America, depending on whether part-time students were counted.

Explanations for the increase lay in the burgeoning baby-boom population and the growing proportion of students who were attending college. From 1960 to 1970, the state's population grew by 21 percent; the number graduating from high school grew by 59 percent. Other explanations lay in continuing prosperity, in the growing demands of employers for well-trained personnel, and in Elkins' standards that caused students to choose College Park over other institutions in the state. More generally, explanations for growth may have lain in the growing complexity of modern life, the excitement of the space age, the fears of the Cold War, the fear of the draft. In any case, a college education—and the best one possible—had become central to the middle class respectability to which almost everyone aspired. Universities were becoming not just a product of the nation's well-being, but a source of it.

Certain colleges within the University grew faster than others, altering the mood within the institution. The number of full-time graduate students grew from 19 percent of the total enrollment in 1954 to 22 percent in 1970, their numbers adding intensity and purposefulness to the campus. Undergraduates were shifting from technical to general education, especially into the growing College of Arts and Sciences. The Colleges of Education and Business were also growing, but Agriculture, Home Economics, Engineering, and Physical Education fell behind. Growth in the Baltimore professional schools and growth in off-campus and adult-education courses was generally slower than at College Park.

State planners were well aware of the surging rise of higher education; occasionally someone liked to talk of hundreds of thousands of students at College Park in the decades. Planners alerted the successive Maryland governors and the General Assembly, and they in turn mobilized citizen commissions for advice. In 1947, a Governor's commission, the Marbury Commission, accurately predicted the enrollments and warned of the costs for future decades. A General Assembly commission of 1955, the Pullen Commission, called for a rise in the number of community colleges, and the state promptly increased their number from three to nine. In 1960,

67. Registration in the Armory was usually a madhouse that lasted for nearly a week each semester.

the Warfield Commission offered a badly received recommendation that all of the state colleges become branches of the University. Two years later, the Curlett Commission persuaded the state to increase the number of community colleges again, from twelve to twenty-three, and to create a permanent Advisory Council for Higher Education to plan for and coordinate the state's institutions.

68. Commencement in Cole Field House, 1964.

Major Construction, 1955-1970

1954   Cole Activities Building, 12,000 seats, $3,250,000. William P. Cole was a regent.

1956   Journalism, $391,000.
        President's House, $61,000.

1957   North Administration, later Mitchell Building, $614,000. Clarence Mitchell was a civil rights leader.

1958   Golf Course, 200,000.
        McKeldin Library, $2.8 million. Theodore R. McKeldin was governor.
        Cecil, Frederick, Dorchester, Worcester Dorms, $1.4 million.

1961   Business and Public Administration, later Tydings Hall, $1.7 million. Millard E. Tydings was a United States senator.
        Foreign Languages, later Jiminez, $510,000. Juan Ramon Jiminez had been a faculty member.
        Cambridge Dorm, $1.1 million.

1962   Cumberland, Chestertown, Centreville, Bel Air Dorms, $4.8 million.

1963   Stamp Student Union addition, $2.1 million.
        Infirmary, later Health Center, $460,000.
        Lord Calvert Apartments, later Graduate Gardens, $1.3 million.
        Computer and Space Science, $310,000.

1964   Physics addition, $3.7 million.
        Center for Adult Education, later University College, $1.6 million.
        Denton Dorm, $1.7 million.

1965   Tawes Fine Arts, $2.8 million.
        College of Education, later Benjamin Building, $1.8 million.

1966   Elkton Dorm, $1.9 million.

1967   Ellicott Dorm, $2.9 million.
        Computer and Space Sciences, $1.5 million.

1968   Cyclotron, $4 million.
        Hagerstown Dorm, $2 million.

1969   South Administration, later Lee Building, $1.2 million. Blair Lee was a governor.
        LaPlata Dorm, $2.3 million.
        University Hills, graduate apartments, $2.1 million.

1970   Animal Sciences, $1.8 million.

The University's first initiative in controlling enrollment was the creation of a branch campus, awkwardly called UMBC, the University of Maryland, Baltimore County. The expansion was popular; state appropriations were generous. Elkins's assistant, Albin O. Kuhn, headed the new campus, and several College Park faculty agreed to transfer there. The first 760 freshmen entered in 1966, and by 1970 the new campus had

Quality and Quantity

3,000 students, most of whom would have otherwise come to College Park. More significant was the determination to cap College Park enrollment by limiting freshman admissions. At the time, it seemed radical to deny admission to graduates of the state's high schools, but this was the step—probably more than any other—that confirmed Elkins's drive toward quality and set the University on a path toward excellence. Beginning in the fall of 1969, College Park accepted graduates only from the top half of their high school class. Other students could transfer in only after they had proved themselves in state or community colleges. During the first year, the policy cut enrollment by an estimated 1,500 students. As had happened before, the tougher the admission standards, the more students wanted in. Enrollment was soon increasing again, and as even more students clamored for entry, the higher the standards could rise.

THE ORIGINS OF DISCONTENT

On the surface, the 1950s and most of the 1960s was a golden age for higher education, but there were other trends beneath the surface. The civil rights movement was growing, the war in Vietnam was expanding, and there was a growing restlessness on American campuses. In 1964, a Free Speech Movement rocked the University of California, Berkeley; in 1968, anti-war protests shut down Columbia University; and in 1970, the National Guard killed four students at Kent State University and two at Jackson State University.

At first, no one paid much attention. College Park administrators, when they noticed the growing discontent on their own campus, dismissed it as the product of too-rapid expansion—the impersonality of a large institution, the loss of campus community, the pressure of rising standards, the large classes, the professors who were too busy with their research. These may have been factors, but discontent was far larger than that; it was as evident in small colleges as in large ones.

Partly, the discontent at College Park came from two decades of prosperity, the rise of larger numbers into the middle class, the demands of ever more people for ever larger autonomy, and the growing opportunity for minorities to express themselves. Partly it came from idealism, itself a product of prosperity, and the belief in equality for minorities, and then demand for the equality of all people. Partly it came from the anger that follows idealism, anger about the war in Vietnam, and then anger against all authority. University enrollment was usually a haven from the military draft during the Vietnam War, and possibly draft evasion, or guilt

69. During the 1960s, the University was constructing one high-rise dormitory every year.

70. Most students from the 1950s to the 1990s were commuters.

over draft evasion, fueled the protests. In any case, the protests grew because they were exciting and because they succeeded so well.

Elkins's first taste of protest came in 1955, when he banned drinking in the dormitories, but squashing that was easy. Occasionally, in the next few years, students circulated petitions against housemothers who were too strict or professors who were too eccentric. There was an alumni protest in 1959, enlisting a few members of the General Assembly, upset that the University seemed to have forgotten Curley Byrd and was losing too many football games. These kinds of protests only strengthened the drive toward quality, advertising excellence and making admission into the University more desirable, but these protests were only a prelude to something much larger.

The first swell of 1960s unrest was the broad, soft protest against *in loco parentis*, the long-standing practice by which the University served as parents who dictated the dress, behavior, and living arrangements of its children. The University yielded slowly, for conservative parents often liked the regulations. One by one, however, the regulations lapsed—rules requiring women to wear skirts to class, curfew rules for dormitories, rules about class attendance, about drinking, about entering dormitories occupied by members of the opposite sex. The students had mostly won by 1970; the administration had lost; and the students were simultaneously empowered and alienated from whatever was the system.

Students led the protests of the 1960s, but the faculty, too, were restless and sometimes egged the students on. The growth of faculty government and autonomy stimulated the demand for still more autonomy. The increasing emphasis on research as the main criteria for advancement allowed non-publishing faculty to claim that the rules had changed. The shrinking academic job market drove nontenured faculty to desperation and anger.

Both students and faculty wanted to make it their own university. In 1966, students launched a "free university" in which faculty or students offered noncredit lectures and discussions, sometimes extending over several weeks, on topics of current interest. Students began a course guide, published more or less annually over the next decade, reviewing departments, courses, and professors, often scathingly, and usually with considerable accuracy.

The largest assertion of student autonomy was the counterculture, flaunting the establishment with irreverence. When incoming freshmen were asked to define themselves as primarily vocational, academic, social, or nonconformist, 19 percent claimed they were primarily nonconformist, and they were the ones who defined the times, who most influenced others. Hippie attitudes and fashions spread—long hair, short skirts, beards, sandals, beads, no bras.

Fraternities and sororities, once centers of rebellion, had become bastions of conformity. Fraternity-sorority membership declined sharply, reaching a nadir in 1970 that included only 11 percent of the undergraduates.

Students adorned the residence halls with posters, mainly of political slogans and rock stars. Some critics have emphasized the importance of rock music that brought together African-American and country culture, that actively promoted civil rights, and that promoted rejection of all authority. In any case, the music grew ever louder, once-forbidden words became commonplace, the smell of marijuana pervaded even the classrooms. Birth control pills came into common use; sex became more casual. It was the day of Haight-Ashbury, the commune, shared possessions, Woodstock 1969, Bob Dylan, the Beatles, drugs, psychedelic and exotic symbols. Head shops in College Park sold bongs, hash pipes, hookas, peace symbols, buttons with political slogans.

Alienation, idealism, and intensity all blended together. Through most of the 1960s, the main political cause was civil rights. In 1960, African-American students led the way, supported by their white friends, with a sit-in at a segregated College Park bowling alley. The bowling alley yielded, and during the next three years, student sit-ins succeeded in integrating most of the nearby stores and restaurants. Protests in neighboring col-

71. A mostly African-American protest group on the steps of the Administration Building, 1972.

72. The campus in 1966.

leges were even louder. In 1963, police arrested 413 sit-in students, mostly from Morgan State College, and the next year, police attacks caused the hospitalization of sixty students at Princess Anne. In 1960, the University forbade the Congress of Racial Equality (CORE) from establishing a chapter on campus, but there were student rallies, and it appeared anyway. It changed its name to the Black Student Union (BSU), and became a center of protest, mostly against racism, but also against poverty and against authority of any sort.

Idealism evolved into anger. The 1964 riots at the University of California, Berkeley, caused millions of dollars of damage, and the 1968 upheaval at Columbia University nearly destroyed that institution. Faculty and students at College Park began calling themselves New Left, or Radicals, often openly embracing violence. The College Park movement centered in the Students for a Democratic Society (SDS), from time to time banned from campus, but ubiquitous after 1967, with pamphlets, loudspeakers and rallies. Mainly the SDS raged against the war in Vietnam, but it embraced rage of any sort.

The University of Maryland at College Park, A History

In April 1968, Martin Luther King was assassinated, and riots spread over American cities. College Park students saw the glow from the fires in Washington and watched 11,600 troops moving along Route One to the Capital. There were 5,310 arrests in Washington, 5,512 in Baltimore. Two weeks later, when President Elkins tried to speak at a campus convocation, the BSU, the SDS, and various supporters blew kazoos and waved banners and walked out. They were not protesting anything in particular that Elkins had done or failed to do, but they were angry, and whatever Elkins said did not much matter.

During the 1968-1969 academic year, the University made mighty efforts to appear accommodating, and briefly the protests seemed to moderate. The administration ended its futile attempt to censor student publications and approved mixed-sex dormitories. The University Senate expanded the right of students and the press to attend its deliberations and approved the first courses in Black Studies. Elkins announced that he would appoint a chancellor to provide new leadership for College Park. All these things were successful in their way, but campus discontent was far deeper, merely dormant, not to be appeased. Larger explosions lay ahead.

CHAPTER IX

Riots and Reorganizations of the 1970s

At College Park, campus discontent blazed into violence, and public anger at the violence slowed the healing. The 1970s was a long decade—perhaps from 1968, when discontent mounted, until 1982, when the economy recovered. Beyond the campus, there were assassinations, urban decay and urban riots, Vietnam, Watergate, the criminal indictment of Maryland governors Spiro T. Agnew and Marvin Mandel, corrosive inflation, recession, malaise.

Most colleges and universities in America—even throughout the world—were enduring turmoil, embracing reform, altering their mission, and submitting to outside controls. Universities mostly abandoned their ancient mission of character development, they shifted their curriculum away from theory and toward relevance and vocationalism, and they embraced new goals of access and egalitarianism. Most states organized their institutions of higher education into a system, and then struggled over whether to equalize the institutions or to provide them with separate missions.

THE RIOTS

During the winter, 1969-1970, discontent smoldered: anti-racism, anti-war, anti-regulations, anti-establishment. The emotions were larger than any particular issue. In the spring, the Philosophy Department denied tenure to two non-publishing faculty members who had friends among the discontented. Students, with a few faculty supporters, called for an all-night sit-in in the philosophy building, the Skinner Building. The tenured faculty were there, willing enough to engage in discussion, but the students remained mostly in the basement, playing drums, smoking pot. Then, on March 24, 1970, at 3:30 a.m., police surrounded the building and arrested eighty-seven people for trespassing. A few days later, the University Senate, acting as a committee-of-the-whole, recommended amnesty for the protesters, but Elkins, eager to crush the troublemakers, pressed for convictions. The campus was seething.

A few weeks later, on May 1, as President Nixon widened the Vietnam War into Cambodia, some 4,000 College Park students poured onto Route One, blocking the boulevard all afternoon. It was the lead item on the national news. During the evening, as students began vandalizing stores, Governor Mandel called out 620 police and 500 troops from the National Guard. With bayonets drawn and clouds of tear gas, the troops moved forward. The students, retreating back toward the campus, smashed hun-

73. Campus scene, 1970.

Riots and Reorganizations of the 1970s

74. Campus scene, 1971.

dreds of windows, set fires in the Administration Building, and fed the fires with the portraits of former University presidents that hung on the walls. There were injuries, especially of students who were gassed and guardsmen hit by rocks. When Elkins announced that the University was closed, five hundred faculty with 7,000 student observers met in the field house. The faculty voted to censure Elkins, and he rescinded the closure, but classes for the remaining five weeks were essentially over. Students generally received the grades they had earned when the month began.

The next fall was tense, with classroom buildings regularly emptied because of bomb threats. The protests were smaller than the year before, but the angry core was more focused. The following May, after major peace demonstrations in Washington, students again blocked Route One, smashed more campus windows, broke furniture, and destroyed trees and shrubbery. Again the National Guard came, this time camping for a week in the Administration Building and making almost 100 arrests. At commencement that year, Madison Jones, the longhaired student government president, addressed the graduates draped in a Vietcong flag.

Still, protest continued. In April 1972, protest organizers were no longer able to mount mass rallies, but there remained hundreds of sympathizers, enough to rampage, throwing rocks and trashing the lobbies of classroom buildings. The National Guard came for a third time and made another seventy arrests. That, finally, was about the end. The war was winding down, radicalism was waning, anger was giving way to resignation, to a stay-cool, hippie ethic, and perhaps, most of all, to economic recession.

We still debate the meaning of the riots: three years in a row, armed forces were necessary to protect the University from the insurrection of its students, often encouraged by the faculty. The student violence damaged property and lives. In the near term, it seemed to point leftward toward weakened formality and authority, toward egalitarianism and democracy; it probably hastened the end of the war in Vietnam. In a longer perspective, the moral fervor and anti-authoritarianism may have pointed rightward, toward religious fundamentalism and more limited government. The particulars of change—the pluses and the minuses—were especially evident in higher education.

REORGANIZATIONS

Everyone in authority was looking for solutions to the problem of discontent, and one of the main academic results was surging bureaucracy. From national, state, University System, and campus levels came new

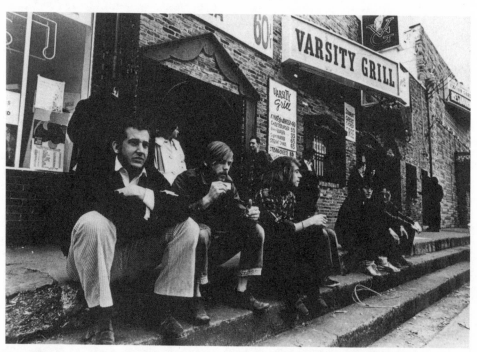

75. Students hang out in College Park, 1971.

guidelines, bureaus, and control—always in the name of accountability and reform, often beneficial, but always intrusive on campus autonomy.

First were the good intentions of the United States Department of Health, Education and Welfare (HEW) in promoting equity for minorities and women. By 1970, the government was establishing goals and then quotas for the employment of minority faculty, and the quotas often exceeded the availability of candidates for the positions. The government scrutinized salary equity for minorities and women, and these salaries increased significantly. HEW brought suits for discrimination against the University, all of which failed.

The state government, although overwhelmingly hostile to student activism, also tried appeasement, lowering the voting age and drinking age in 1974 from 21 to 18. Student voting rates remained low, however, far below those of their elders. For a while the University served beer in the dining halls, but in 1982 the General Assembly raised the drinking age back to 21.

The State Board for Higher Education assumed increasing authority to influence budgets and approve new academic programs. Intermittently through the 1970s, the Board frowned on the preeminence of the College Park campus, worked to equalize its teaching loads and salaries with the state colleges, and sought to block new programs or to transfer existing ones to weaker institutions. The Board sent questionnaires to all faculty asking them to account for their time, hour by hour.

Elkins and the regents, meanwhile, were launching their own reorganization—a chancellor system. Elkins and his staff would supervise the five campuses (College Park, University College, Baltimore, Baltimore County, and Eastern Shore), with a chancellor for each. A College Park chancellor search committee worked through the unrest in the spring of 1970 and came up with a candidate, Charles Edwin Bishop, whom Elkins accepted. Elkins moved off-campus to University College; later the System office moved farther away, to a new building named for Elkins. All of this was an essential fresh start in a time of troubles, but a president plus a chancellor provided another layer of administration. Bureaucracy expanded as public favor and public support contracted.

Bishop dominated the campus from 1970 to 1974, launching the greatest reorganization of all. He had grown up poor in the hill-country of South Carolina, was a noted agricultural economist and was a vice president at the University of North Carolina. He was truly egalitarian, as the times required, and he was ambitious to do big things in the world. People usually liked his goals, and he was generally successful in attaining them, but, in these times, no one in authority was very popular. He selected from the faculty a team of four vice chancellors—one for academic affairs, one for academic planning and innovations, one for business affairs, and one for student affairs.

Bishop changed the academic calendar, in part to shorten the springtime riot season. Instead of running from September to June, the calendar extended from August to May. Bishop encouraged the University Senate to reorganize itself, eliminating the representatives from other campuses, reducing the number of administrators, and adding students and staff to its membership.

Bishop's main reorganization plan for College Park took almost two years, through committees, through the new College Park Campus Senate, through Elkins and the regents. It called for five provosts: one for Agricultural and Life Sciences, one for Arts and Humanities (and Architecture and Journalism), one for Behavioral and Social Sciences (and Business), one for Mathematical and Physical Sciences and Engineering, and a miscellaneous provost for everything else (Education, Home Economics,

76. Chancellor Charles E. Bishop and three vice chancellors: John W. Dorsey, Administrative Affairs; George H. Callcott, Academic Affairs; Thomas B. Day, Academic Planning and Policy.

Riots and Reorganizations of the 1970s

Library Science, Physical Education). The plan aimed at relevance, bringing theory and application together, and it aimed at decentralization, moving management away from the administration building. For a decade, it worked adequately, but it was not an educational revolution. The disciplines and professions benefited from their close association, but they never really warmed to their marriage; and what Bishop saw as decentralization downward to five provosts, the departments and colleges saw as centralization upward into an additional layer of bureaucracy.

REFORMS

Other reforms of the early 1970s were less ambitious and more successful. One of the greatest and least noticed was computerized registration, the product of technology. Before 1970, registration took up most of a week as students stood in lines, searched out each professor they wanted, and looked for another class if the one they wanted was full. Now, each professor's teaching schedule was available weeks in advance, and students online could complete the process in an hour. Deans could monitor the enrollment, adding courses or canceling them. Students took what they wanted instead of what professors wanted to teach, and everyone saved a week of time.

Searching for flexibility and relevance, Bishop and the Senate relaxed course requirements and grading practices. Basic requirements dropped from twelve courses in specific subjects to ten courses, mostly unspecified, mainly ensuring wide distribution over the disciplines. To reduce grade pressure, the University allowed students to drop courses at almost any time and to take certain courses with grades of Pass or Fail. Many faculty members, on their own, reduced grade pressure even more by raising grades from an average of C, which had prevailed in the 1950s, to an average near B in the mid-1970s. The priority of academic rigor gave way to the priority of student comfort. Students were customers in an academic supermarket.

Bishop and the Senate established a Dean for Undergraduate Studies to enrich the undergraduate experience—to promote better student advising, more interdisciplinary programs, and varied educational experiences. Attempts to require all faculty to serve as advisors failed, for many professors resented the assignment. Instead, departments and colleges employed student peer advisors along with full-time professional advisors, and this worked nicely. To promote interdisciplinary study, students, with the dean's approval, could design their own major. To promote relevance with the outside world, students could obtain credit for supervised, off-campus internships, usually in government or business offices. The honors program grew, with special courses and independent study for able students. Orientation programs expanded, both for students and for parents.

Athletics was another way of appealing to students. Fortuitously, just before Bishop arrived, James H. Kehoe became Athletic Director. Kehoe attracted Charles G. "Lefty" Driesell to coach basketball, and three years later hired Jerry Claiborne to coach football. More than at any time since the early 1950s, Maryland sports were big-time. Four times in the next ten years, Driesell's teams ranked among the top ten in the country. Six of his players were All-American: Tom McMillen, John Lucas, Len Elmore, Albert King, Buck Williams, and Len Bias. McMillen was the University's first Rhodes Scholar. During Claiborne's ten years at Maryland, his teams won 77, lost 37, and tied 3, with seven trips to bowl games: Peach (1973), Liberty (1974), Gator (1915), Cotton (1976), Hall of Fame (1977), Sun (1978), and Tangerine (1980). In women's athletics, Chris Weller became basketball coach in 1975, and her teams were immediately among the best in the country. All of this promoted pride on the campus, a partial balance to discontent.

Almost everyone in the early 1970s seemed to be looking for ways to recruit and serve the growing number of African-American students—HEW offered money and quotas, the State Board for Higher Education issued mandates, and Bishop and the College Park Campus Senate were fully sympathetic to the cause. The result was more bureaucracy: an Office of Equal Opportunity Office Recruitment, an Upward Bound program to help minority students adjust to college, an Intensive Educational Program to provide special tutoring for disadvantaged students, and a Nyumburu Cultural Center that provided a meeting place and supervised activities for African-Americans. A Human Relations Office listened to grievances, promoted understanding between contesting parties, and pressed toward equity.

Women's protest organizations grew as loud as those of African-Americans, and the administration's response was faster. A Women's Studies Program developed, with its first course in 1971 and over thirty courses five years later. Consciousness raising was rapid and genuine. Disciplines like English, history, and government incorporated feminist ways of thinking, and mostly male-dominated fields like engineering and the sciences actively recruited women students.

By 1979, the number of male undergraduates still exceeded females, 52 percent to 48 percent, but, for the next few years, female graduate stu-

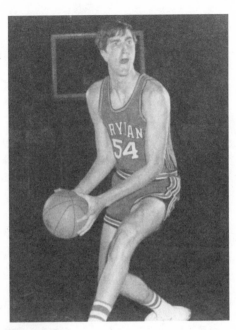

77. Rhodes Scholar, Tom McMillen

78. Basketball Coach, "Lefty" Driesell.

dents exceeded males by the same margin. Presumably, about as many women as men were entering the college-level workforce. Surely this marked a social revolution, a reversal of centuries of custom. The proportion of women on the College Park faculty increased from 17 percent in 1968 to 26.5 percent in 1982.

The student mood, however, at least during the early 1970s, remained rebellious and angry. Pictures in the student yearbook were of police attacking students, graffiti, littered streets, smashed automobiles, empty rooms, guns, wounded animals, filthy toilets, death masks. Beatnik-hippie living arrangements reached a peak, with communes spreading into nearby Berwyn and Hyattsville. Students liked old cars, painted with peace signs and psychedelic colors. They explored occult religion. Anger promoted crime. In 1971, the Federal Bureau of Investigation cited College Park as the fifth most crime-ridden campus in the country. The severe unhappiness was brief, but it was real and deep.

The country's urban centers were the other major source of anger, and University officials, fearing a melding of urban and campus disorder, blocked the Washington area Metro's planned station on the campus. This was an action the University would later much regret.

According to Counseling Center surveys, marijuana smoking peaked about 1974, when over 60 percent of the incoming students reported smoking pot occasionally, and 37 percent smoked it regularly. No doubt, the number was far higher for more senior students. About 11 percent of the freshmen had experimented with hallucinogenic drugs or cocaine. Marijuana and hallucinogenic drug use declined through the rest of the decade, although cocaine use increased slightly. Of course, there were always traditional and conservative students as well, especially in business and engineering.

By mid-decade, the student mood was shifting dramatically, even reversing itself—from political commitment to apathy, from idealism to self-indulgence, from anger to pessimism. Political slogans disappeared, the new fad phrase was "stay cool." Almost everyone embraced the new ideal of equality for the sexes and races, although translating the rhetoric into reality would be long and arduous. Sexual permissiveness prevailed, gays and lesbians came out and usually gained acceptance. The most active political organization was MaryPIRG, the Maryland Public Interest Research Group, founded by Ralph Nader and dedicated to research into corporate wrongdoing. Religious fundamentalists distributed tracts.

People began calling it the "Me Decade." Angry rock music turned to disco; students began wearing expensive clothing and gold jewelry. Head shops turned themselves into health food shops; a food co-op appeared in the Student Union. Pinball machines, skateboards and jogging became fashionable. For a moment in the mid-1970s, there was a fad for streaking, students running naked over the campus.

Faculty culture was also changing during the 1970s—away from hierarchy, toward democracy, politicization, and ultimately toward disengagement. Chancellor Bishop made department "heads" into "chairmen"; then, on second thought, into "chairpersons," and then "chairs." Over the decade, most departments adopted by-laws that made the chairs essentially elective, usually for a term of about five years. The tenured faculty, rather than the chairs, assumed most authority for recommending appointments and promotions. Elected committees assumed most authority for awarding salary increases. The first result of this democratization was good, for colleagues were generally bolder, more rigorous in promoting excellence, and more astute in judgment than department heads had been. It may, however, have pushed colleagues into a heightened competition, and thus lessened departmental cohesion.

Until the 1960s, the authority of the president, deans, and department chairs had prevailed. They were joined by a handful of faculty stars— George Snow and Richard Ferrell in physics, Charles Schultze and Mancur Olson in economics, Carl Bode in English, Peter Lejins in sociology, Tom Aylward in speech. The administrators and stars provided a campus community, chaired the main committees, lunched in the faculty club, and

79. Streaking, 1974.

admitted promising lesser faculty into their counsels. Rank prevailed, although tensions were growing in departments and across the campus, mainly between the establishment and the younger faculty.

By the 1970s, the campus establishment was fading. For a while, it seemed that everyone wanted to run the University. During the riots, faculty coalitions emerged—a small radical coalition (maybe twenty or so) that related to the SDS, a large reformist coalition (including 500 or more) that leaned leftward but opposed disruption, smaller coalitions (maybe of 200 or more, centered in the professional colleges) that embraced tradition, and a remaining contingent (500 or more) that withdrew from the contention. This was similar to divisions found in other major universities.

As faculty politics intensified, departmental tensions grew—not mainly by age as in the past, but also by field, and by views on campus and world affairs. Democracy prevailed as the only means of maintaining order. As authority declined, as the respect for seniority and eminence diminished, campus community weakened.

Also there was gender change. The faculty of the 1960s was still mostly male. Their female spouses, mostly without separate careers, hosted dinner parties and picnics for their husbands' departmental colleagues. By the 1970s, the wives of faculty members were increasingly professionals themselves, and sometimes the spouses of faculty members were men. Most departments were actively recruiting women, and male and female faculty members easily resented biases that they perceived toward the other. Departmental parties and picnics almost ended.

Enrollment in the 1970s flowed out of traditional subjects like English, history, and mathematics. It surged especially into psychology, which, for a while during the mid-1970s, was the hottest subject, where students analyzed themselves and each other. Enrollment also moved into vocational fields that promised employment, especially engineering, business, journalism, architecture, and the newly established fields of computer science and criminology. New programs grew in African-American Studies, Women's Studies, and geology.

New buildings, mostly authorized in the decade before, altered the face of the campus—the Zoology-Psychology Building in 1971, Architecture in 1971, Hornbake Library in 1971, Health and Human Performance in 1973, Art-Sociology Building in 1976, and an addition to Human Ecology in 1981. The buildings provided space for crowded departments, but since maintenance budgets hardly changed, the luxury of space was almost matched by a feeling of strained resources and constraint. Offices were seldom cleaned; faculty placed their wastebaskets in the hallways for a weekly pickup.

Riots and Reorganizations of the 1970s

Major Construction, 1971-1976

1971   Zoology-Psychology, later Biology-Psychology, $7.3 million
        Architecture, $1.7 million.
        Leonardtown Dorm, $1.6 million.
1972   Undergraduate Library, later Hornbake Library, $8.1 million. R. Lee
         Hornbake was a former vice president.
1973   Health and Human Performance, additions to 1981, total $9.9 million
1974   South Campus Dining, $5 million.
1976   Art-Sociology, $6 million.
        [There was no major construction from 1976 to 1988]

Riots, reorganization, and reforms were nearly over by 1974, but still the campus was far from happy. In dollar terms, the costs of change had far outdistanced new revenues. The public, the governor, and the General Assembly were unfriendly toward higher education generally, which seemed to be the center of social unrest, and especially unsympathetic toward the riotous state university. In the early 1970s, enrollments declined slightly and inflation-adjusted budgets declined more. The faculty paid much of the price because, for the moment, faculty mobility was greatly diminished, for there were few jobs elsewhere. It would take time for prosperity to return, for malaise to fade.

BISHOP, DORSEY, AND GLUCKSTERN

After four years in College Park, Bishop announced his departure. Perhaps he was weary of the turmoil or frustrated by Elkins's continuing oversight, or perhaps he knew that campus executives usually make their major contribution within the first few years of their administration. In any case, he had an offer to head the system of higher education in Arkansas. For ten months, John Dorsey served as acting chancellor. He had been an undergraduate at College Park, obtained a Ph.D. from Harvard, returned as Professor of Economics, and was Bishop's efficient and easygoing vice chancellor for administrative affairs. He promoted harmony and marked the beginnings of adjustment, respite.

In the fall of 1975, Robert L. Gluckstern succeeded Dorsey as chancellor. He was a graduate of City College in New York, a professor of physics at Yale, and then provost at the University of Massachusetts. He was ideal for a time of healing—a calm manager, friendly, relaxed, candid, happy to accept changes from the recent past but generally lacking an agenda for more change. Bishop, as the early 1970s demanded, emphasized teaching and student services; Gluckstern, as the late 1970s permitted, shifted gently back toward faculty interests and research.

Gluckstern proceeded deliberately to expand access, to make the campus more diverse. He launched the Banneker Scholarships, named after an African-American scientist, that eventually attracted each year to the campus about 40 high-achieving African-American students. He initiated a Golden ID program to allow people over age 60 to take courses free of charge. Many joined the program, mostly retired people, often with advanced degrees, and usually they were among the best students in a class. Prompted by federal legislation, the administration installed elevators, automatic door openers, and ramps for the disabled.

The largest of these new programs, required by the federal law known as Title IX, brought increased urgency to the search for equality among men and women. The federal government, the campus, and the departments all established committees that searched for inequities. The administration provided for family-related leaves. Gluckstern set aside for women and minorities a large portion of the vacancies that occurred, and many of his administrative positions went to them.

The big Title IX problem was in athletics, and Gluckstern pushed ahead against the macho and largely independent Department of Intercollegiate Athletics. Although the athletic program received most of its funding from gate receipts and alumni contributions, Gluckstern moved toward an equal or equitable number of athletic scholarships for men and women, and toward equal or equitable funding for their coaches and teams that the law required. The extra costs were covered by new athletic fees required of all students. Women participated in athletics as never before, expanding a dimension of their life, enriching campus life, offering new fodder for sports page editors.

Efforts also continued to improve teaching and recognize good teachers. The Distinguished Scholar-Teacher program recognized annually about six outstanding faculty who received a modest stipend and delivered a public lecture. A Distinguished University Professor program provided an extra rank and world-class salaries for a handful of campus stars. The Honors Program expanded. A Chancellor's Scholars program actively recruited outstanding high school seniors, offering scholarships based on attainment rather than need.

The College of Business and Management was the fastest-growing academic program in the late 1970s, raising its standards and doubling in size within a decade, integrating with the business world, imparting to the campus a spirit of entrepreneurship. A new School of Public Affairs appeared

Riots and Reorganizations of the 1970s

80. Robert L. Gluckstern, Chancellor, 1975-1982.

in 1981, partly staffed by high-ranking, out-of-office Washington officials, largely funded by research grants, and limited to graduate students.

Early in 1978, President Wilson Elkins retired after sixteen years as president at College Park and eight more years as president of the five-campus system. Admired for building quality during his early years, he had become a symbol of conservatism and stability. His successor as head of the University system was John S. Toll—"Johnny" to most people—head of the University's Physics Department from 1953 to 1965 and the greatest department head the University had ever had; then, from 1965 to 1978, a successful builder of the State University of New York at Stony Brook. Toll arrived like a whirlwind, demanding that College Park aspire to excellence, demanding that it integrate with the state and become the engine of its economy, demanding that it become one of the ten great public universities in the nation.

People discounted the ebullience, or failed to understand it, but it was the beginning of a new rhetoric and energy for the University. At once, Toll was off in every direction, sometimes ignoring Gluckstern and his successors, promoting campus initiatives, finding new money and research grants. When Gluckstern recommended a Marxist, Bertram Ollman, as chair of the Government Department, Toll rejected the appointment. As long as Toll served, there were two leaders for the College Park campus.

Despite Toll's optimism, a blighting economic cloud hung over the

81. John S. Toll, President of the University System, 1978-1989.

campus, worsening as the 1970s went on. The pall hung over all of higher education, but College Park especially felt the gloom. The riots had been costly, the reorganizations and reforms had been more costly still. The public and General Assembly remained unfriendly, for a while inflation passed ten percent a year, and the recession of 1978-1982 was the worst in forty years.

"Accountability" and "retrenchment" became the watchwords of administrators. The University squeezed income from students and from research grants, but as state appropriations declined, faculty and students paid the price. From 1970 to 1982, the number of faculty remained approximately the same, but evermore positions were assigned to administration. Faculty salaries in those years rose 81 percent, but the consumer price index rose 61 percent, so for over a decade, real faculty income increased only slightly. Student tuition rose 120 percent, room and board 165 percent.

The story was similar for all of higher education, but it was especially vivid at College Park. The 1970s had brought a wave of democracy, both its violence and its reforms. Maybe it was a revolution. Along the way came economic recession. Gluckstern calmed the storm, curtailing the excesses, but in 1982, after seven years as chancellor, he wanted to become a physicist again.

It was time for a new story, time for the economy to recover, time for Toll's vision to catch on.

CHAPTER X

Aspiring in the 1980s

The University took some stumbles in the 1980s, but mostly it glowed with expectations. Beyond the campus, President Ronald Reagan radiated confidence, claiming victory in the Cold War and basking in public favor. Computers reshaped American life, middle class prosperity surged. In Maryland, Governors Harry Hughes and William Donald Schaefer grasped the growing importance of higher education and had the revenues to promote it. At College Park, Chancellor John B. Slaughter enjoyed the improved climate, but when basketball hero Len Bias died from an overdose of cocaine, Slaughter struggled in vain to gain control over intercollegiate athletics. Then came the new president, William E. Kirwan, exuding optimism.

Throughout the country, American universities were recovering from change and malaise, mainly through a newfound alliance with business. University research was paying off, knowledge was advancing more rapidly then ever, and business was paying for the new knowledge. The economy was beginning to surge, and universities proclaimed themselves the engines of the economy. Back in public favor, enjoying new prosperity, they struggled with their internal problems of racial and gender equity, external system control, and long-standing tensions like those between scholarship and athletics.

John B. Slaughter and the Quality of Campus Life

The new chancellor was, like most political and academic leaders, the symbol as much as the shaper of the times. Slaughter was an African-American, the first to lead a major, mostly white university. Far from controversial, however, the appointment made people feel good; it seemed natural. Times had changed. Slaughter had grown up in Kansas, was pro-

123

fessor of electrical engineering at the University of Washington, provost at Washington State University, and President Jimmy Carter's appointed head of the august National Science Foundation. Slaughter was warm, handsome, courtly, somewhat formal. His language was eloquent, maybe a bit dated, with quotations from the Bible, Shakespeare, Tennyson—all about greatness, opportunity, potential, quality, pride.

His main concern, it turned out, was improving the quality of campus life, making people feel good about themselves, giving faculty and students pride in the University. He was right, morale was a problem in a huge campus emerging from turmoil, recently wracked by racial-class-gender-ideological conflict. His very concern promoted good feelings, and the rising prosperity helped. He spoke of making the University "a personal, caring place," of giving people "a sense of mission in helping others."

Slaughter's related concern, even more than for his predecessors, was for expanding opportunities for minorities. Since that sounded paternalistic, the new euphemism was promoting diversity. Slaughter went personally to mostly black high schools and churches to recruit students, to inform them about the expanding types of student aid that were available. The proportion of undergraduate African-Americans rose from 7.6 percent in 1980 to 10.8 percent in 1990, one of the highest proportions of any state university in the country. The escalating efforts by Chancellors

82. John B. Slaughter, Chancellor, 1982-1988.

Aspiring in the 1980s

Bishop, Gluckstern, and Slaughter to help minorities were increasingly successful, even if, in the process, the state's predominantly black colleges were losing their best students.

Slaughter was the first campus executive since Curley Byrd who really liked the company of students. In the evening, he toured the residence halls and the fraternity and sorority houses to talk, not to make speeches, but to engage in dialogue about learning and life. He promoted awards ceremonies and wrote endless letters of congratulations. He was concerned about academic retention, ordered studies about student dropouts, and urged the deans to reach out to their weakest students. In 1980, 43 percent of the entering freshmen were graduating within five years; in 1990, 51 percent were graduating in that time.

The upbeat student mood of the 1980s was a product of much more than anything that Slaughter did. Along with prosperity, there was the pendulum swing of reaction to the recent past. Hippies became yuppies. The new fashion was for vocationalism, jobs, and success. It was once again fashionable to relish campus life, join organizations, cheer the team, boast of campus spirit. The yearbook, *Terrapin*, provided annual portfolios of campus beauty—cherry trees in the spring, shady mall walks in summer, maples in the fall, snowfall in winter. Homecomings, cheerleaders, bonfires were back in style. Jim Henson, a College Park graduate and a frequent speaker on campus, was providing one of the decade's most popular television shows, "Sesame Street," whose main characters were the muppets.

The campus sparkled with new life. The refurbished Student Union, renamed the Adele H. Stamp Student Union, opened pleasant shops and a bank. The Art Attack was a huge, springtime mall festival of student creativity. The Medieval Mercenary Militia wore costumes and undertook mock battles. Students displayed a half-acre-sized AIDS quilt to memorialize friends who had died. The College Park shopping area, although never glittering, regained some life with the refurbished 'Vous, the Maryland Book Exchange, Bentley's, Santa Fe, Kinko's.

Spring Break became a tradition, the University acknowledging it with a longer spring holiday. The break reflected the new prosperity that would grow in succeeding decades. All winter, the beach hotels of Florida and Mexico flooded the campus with flyers offering enticing package deals. Hundreds of students took off for days in the sun, drinking beer, enjoying more hedonism than the campus allowed.

Happy students and satisfied parents were the main impetus behind a new curriculum reform. Universities regularly change their basic require-

83. The Campus Beautiful, 1986.

ments every few decades as needs and fashions change. Now, in the 1980s, people wanted more requirements, more rigor. Faculty committees deliberated. The results were complex, but the number of required courses increased from ten to nineteen. Students would take three courses in basic English and math, nine courses widely distributed over the disciplines, six courses in advanced studies outside their major, and one course in a culture outside the mainstream, mainly black, women's, or Jewish studies. The day of the general survey was passed, sampling was taking its place.

Slaughter—or the changing mood of the 1980s—served the faculty, mostly through rising salaries. Most faculty obtained computers on their desks. The faculty was especially pleased as library holdings increased and as the library catalogue became available online. An expanded Center for Young Children, operated by the College of Education, offered daycare for faculty and staff families. Slaughter reinstituted a faculty-staff convocation—abandoned since the 1960s—conducted in the chapel rather than in the field house, with organ music and academic robes, dedicated to recognizing faculty and staff who had made outstanding contributions. A Chancellor's Medal went to an especially distinguished honoree, who made the main address of the day.

More substantial as a means of pleasing the faculty was the dismantling of the unpopular provost system. Slaughter listened to deans and department chairs who claimed that the system provided an unnecessary level of management; he appointed a committee; he asked the Senate for advice; and he accepted the committee report that the Senate had modified. The process was more important than the product, for the faculty,

84. Spring Break, 1988

with no pressure from the administration, shaped an organization entirely to its wishes. In place of the five divisions that lasted from 1973 to 1986, the campus now had twelve colleges, plus two smaller colleges that called themselves schools. The transition was fairly easy.

The President's Medal
For Outstanding Service to the University (Chancellor's Medal to 1988)

1985   Paul P. Traver, Director Maryland Chorus, Music
1986   Donald Maley, Education
1987   Richard H. Jaquith, Associate Vice Chancellor, Chemistry
1988   J. Robert Dorfman, Provost, Physical Sciences and Technology
         Thomas M. Magoon, Counseling Center
1989   Graciela Nemes, Spanish and Portuguese
1990   Jacob Goldhaber, Provost, Dean of Graduate Studies, Mathematics
1991   Dudley Dillard, Economics
1992   Donald C. Piper, Government and Politics
1993   Margaret Bridwell, Director of Health Services
         Eugenie Clark, Zoology
1994   George H. Callcott, Vice Chancellor for Academic Affairs, History
1996   Robert L. Gluckstern, Chancellor, Physics
         Jack Minker, Computer Science
1997   David Driskell, Art
1998   Marie Davidson, President's Office, Education
         Rudolph P. Lamone, Dean of Business and Management
1999   Ira Berlin, Dean of Undergraduate Studies, History
2000   William L. Thomas, Vice President of Student Affairs, Education
2001   Irwin L. Goldstein, Provost, Dean of Behavioral and Social Sciences,
         Psychology
2002   Charles F. Sturtz, Vice President Administrative Affairs 2003
         Ralph D. Bennett, Jr., Architecture
2004   George E. Dieter, Dean of Engineering, Mechanical Engineering

---

Quality of life also lay in things aesthetic. Landscape architects redesigned the mall in the 1980s, replacing asphalt walkways with concrete and brick; planting willow oak, cherry, and golden chain trees; installing a fountain that became a campus symbol. Landscaping and benches made Hornbake Plaza, Tawes Plaza, and a score of smaller plots into pleasant gathering places. There was money for spring bulbs and summer annuals—daffodils and tulips, pansies, geraniums, begonias, petunias, marigolds, salvia.

Distinguished University Professors
The Highest Academic Rank, created 1980

1980 Mancur Olson, Economics
Samuel Schoenbaum, English
Robert W. Zwanzig, Physical
Sciences and Technology
1981 Louis R. Harlan, History
1988 Michael E. Fischer, Physical
Sciences and Technology
1989 Roald Z. Sagdeev, Physics
Thomas C. Schelling, Economics
1995 Ivo M. Babuska, Mathematics
Stephen G. Brush, History
Guillermo A. Calvo, Economics
Sankar Das Sarma, Physics
David C. Driscoll, Art
Bruce L. Gardner, Agricultural
Economics
Ted Robert Gurr, Government
and Politics
Richard Just, Agricultural
Economics
Edward Ott, Electrical
Engineering
Jose Emilio Pacheco, Foreign
Languages
Azriel Rosenfield, Computer
Engineering
John D. Weeks, Physical Sciences
and Technology
James A. Yorke, Mathematics
1996 Carol S. Carter-Porges, Biology
Elizabeth Gantt, Cell Biology
Serguei Novikov, Physical
Sciences and Technology
Jan V. Sengers, Chemical
Engineering
Richard A. Webb, Physics
1997 Ira Berlin, History
George Gloeckler, Physics
Stanley Plumley, English
Harriet B. Presser, Sociology
Lawrence W. Sherman,
Criminology

1998 Millard H. Alexander, Chemistry
Theodor O. Diener,
Biolosystems Research
James B. Gilbert, History
2000 Michael F. A'Hearn, Physics
Richard A. Etlin, Architecture
Mark I. Freidlin, Mathematics
George H. Lorimer, Chemistry
Ellen D. Williams, Physics
2001 Stuart S. Antman, Mathematics
Benjamin R. Barber,
Government and Pollitics
Eugenia F. Kalnay, Meteorology
William D. Phillips, Physics
George Ritzer, Sociology
Allen Schick, Public Affairs
Katepalli R. Sreenivasan, Physical
Sciences and Technology
Mark Turner, English
2002 Arie W. Kruglanski, Psychology
Howard B. Lasnik, Linguistics
Ramamoorthy Ramesch,
Nuclear Engineering
2004 Rita R. Colwell, Cell Biology
William Hodos, Psychology
Jerrold Levinson, Philosophy

The University of Maryland at College Park, A History

Faculty contentment of the 1980s and 1990s lay partly in their disengagement from the campus, for increasingly, they were finding their colleagues from within their specialty on other campuses, or with business and government agencies with whom they worked. Maybe disengagement from campus affairs came with an increasing concern for research, or with the use of computers and electronic mail, or with general satisfaction with campus affairs. A small group of faculty served in the College Park Campus Senate, and their power to shape policy was very large, but many faculty members, including many of the most renowned, were not much concerned with how the University ran, except for their own working conditions. Faculty club attendance declined. The University's location in the Washington suburbs was a stimulus to professional contacts and research, and location was a major recruiting advantage for the University. Still, most faculty lived far beyond College Park, even outside the county, and campus community suffered.

LEN BIAS, DRUGS, AND ATHLETICS

The University's major stumble of the 1980s came with intercollegiate athletics. Most university presidents pretended not to know what was happening in their athletic departments, but events conspired at Maryland, and Slaughter had to face them. The fact was that big-time athletics was a many-million-dollar business at least partly independent from its own universities; and coaches and athletes worth millions of dollars often had little time left over for things academic.

In 1986, Maryland's Len Bias was probably the best-known player in college basketball, everybody's All-American, the first-round pick of the Boston Celtics, the country's most celebrated professional team. On June 17, after the school year ended, Bias visited Boston and learned that he would be making over a million dollars a year in salary and endorsements. Returning the next day to College Park, he and three basketball friends bought some beer, acquired some cocaine, and went to his room to celebrate. By six o'clock the next morning, he was dead from an overdose. Someone notified Coach Lefty Driesell, and he sent an assistant coach to clean up Bias's room. The University held a memorial service in Cole Field House, where Bias had starred. Over 11,000 people attended. The Reverend Jesse Jackson compared Bias to Jesus and Martin Luther King. Forty television trucks and a hundred reporters descended on the campus. An ambitious county prosecutor, running for office, convened a grand jury to prove that Driesell had obstructed justice with the cleanup and

85. Len Bias, basketball All-American.

that College Park was a drug haven. Reporters discovered the worst—that during the basketball season Bias had completed no courses at all, that his grades and those of most of his teammates were below the level usually required for University retention, and that, incidentally, over the past six years, a majority of the football and basketball players had been admitted as exceptions to the University's published admission standards. Although the athletes were below University standards, they were within standards set by the National Collegiate Athletic Association. Maybe something was wrong with intercollegiate athletics.

President Toll and the regents lay low; Slaughter had to face the world alone. Slaughter loved athletics. Sometimes he joined coaches on recruiting trips and invited recruits and players to his home. He thought of athletics as an avenue for African-Americans to obtain an education. His closeness to the team may have unintentionally emboldened Driesell and the athletic department in their growing excesses. Still, he was distressed to discover the reality of the excesses and especially the players' academic failure. Yes, he said, he had been blind, and he was to blame. The University had been "exploiting" its players. This was the headline across the nation. University presidents in the past and at other campuses regularly boasted of the opportunities they provided for their players. But Slaughter told the truth: big-time athletics was also exploitation.

Slaughter considered radical reform—curtailing athletic scholarships, holding athletes to regular admission standards, restricting freshman play—but this would have sent athletes to rival schools and would have eliminated Maryland from big-time competition. The fact was that the University did not belong to Slaughter and the faculty, but also to students, alumni, and to the people of Maryland. It did not exist for education alone, but also, among other things, for public entertainment.

Slaughter acted as decisively as he could—Maryland would shorten its forthcoming basketball season by two months, it would curtail practices, and it would employ academic and counseling advisors for the players. Slaughter announced the resignation of Richard Dull, the Director of Athletics who had served during the period of the greatest excesses. The larger problem was Coach Lefty Driesell, once so dominant in competition and once concerned for his players, but increasingly challenged on the court, and increasingly demanding of his players. Slaughter hesitated, then announced that Driesell was fired, even though breaking his contract would cost almost a million dollars. Two days later, Slaughter announced that Driesell's successor would be Bob Wade, an African-American from a high school in Baltimore. There had been no search committee for one of the biggest jobs in college basketball, and the Atlantic Coast Conference had never had an African-American coach before.

The publicity over athletic reform was as large as the storm over events that triggered the reform. Newspaper editorials and academic commentators cheered Slaughter's boldness—trying to put education ahead of athletics. But sports writers and boosters were outraged—Slaughter was making Dull and Driesell into scapegoats, and Wade was named because of his race. The boosters were concentrated in the Terrapin Club, the 3,000 alumni and fans who each contributed $125 or more annually to support the athletic program. Club members formed a committee to persuade Toll, the regents, and the governor to fire Slaughter. Passions about athletics mixed with the still more explosive issue of race. Hate mail, often anonymous, rained down on the chancellor. An airplane flew over a Maryland football game with a banner, "Sack Slaughter."

Still, the troubles mounted. If Driesell placed basketball victories over student well-being, the football coach, Bobby Ross, placed victories ahead of sportsmanship. In 1986, after losing a game, Ross raced across the field to attack a referee. The Atlantic Coast Conference banned Ross from the next game. He should have been banned from more. Slaughter issued a reprimand, and Ross resigned. His successor had losing seasons. Hiring Wade, meanwhile, turned out to be a mistake; he was in over his head, unaware of his own recruiting infractions. The National Collegiate Athletic Association investigated and banned Maryland basketball from one year of live television coverage and two years of post-season games.

Most people believed that Maryland had suffered a disastrous setback with the unprecedented publicity over drugs and athletics, especially with the unmentionable issue of race in the background. Actually, however, the University had been forthright about the drugs and athletic excess that everyone knew existed everywhere, and it had been unswerving in its dedication to education of minorities. The University failed in its effort to reform athletics, but at least it seemed to try. State appropriations and applications for admission continued to rise; annual giving dipped briefly, then rose again. The dilemma remained: big-time athletics and academic achievement did not mix easily, and yet they had to accommodate each other. The University had to be excellent in many things.

Contradiction and inclusiveness: that was postmodernism, the way of thinking for a new age, that was the modern university—athletics *and* academics, diversity *and* quality, teaching *and* research, vocationalism *and* the core disciplines, providing knowledge *and* building character, equality *and* elitism, relativism *and* values. Clark Kerr at the University of California popularized the term "multiversity" to encompass the contradictions. Be not dismayed at the University's breadth.

NEW ENTERPRISES

During the 1980s, the state's per capita income rose by 49 percent; student tuition and fees rose 156 percent; research grants rose 218 percent; and state appropriations to the University rose by 236 percent. Inflation accounted for at least one-half of these numbers, but still, per capita income was soaring, and University income was rising twice as fast. For the first time in its history—but not for the last—the University could afford some luxuries, could imagine catching up with the best state universities, could think honestly in terms of excellence.

University officials, especially Toll, were shrewd in their appeals to Governors Hughes and Schaefer and to the General Assembly. Instead of asking mainly for general salary increases, they asked for a lump sum amount that would be used for recruiting outstanding faculty from other institutions or for retaining faculty who received offers from rivals. Much of the recruitment fund went for minorities and women. The retention fund went to about fifty faculty each year, a permanent boost averaging about $5,000 each year. When it came to salaries, Maryland could bid along with the best.

Equally important was gaining control of overhead funds from research grants. Instead of the state collecting almost half of all research grant money for building maintenance and the like, the state agreed to pay overhead costs, remitting the overhead income to the campus in order to promote additional research and additional funding. Research grants increased from $30 million in 1980 to $102 million in 1990. The state's contribution to research thus benefited the nation, elevated the institution, and served as leverage for additional dollars that flowed into the state.

Other appropriations came for scholarships, both for undergraduate and graduate students. Many scholarships were based on need, for need grew as fees rose, but an increasing number were based on merit. Scholarships raised the quality of the students and the reputation of the University.

Still other appropriations came for specific academic programs that were contributing most to the state's economy—especially computer science, engineering, and business. Each of these was an epic of academic growth, public service, and social impact.

The greatest of the new programs was computer science. Computers first became important in weapons research during World War II. During the 1950s, College Park faculty doing research in mathematics, physics, and engineering began renting time on huge electronic vacuum circuit UNIVAC machines owned by the Department of Defense. In 1958, the College of Engineering acquired the first digital machine on the campus; the dean would loan the key to a faculty member for a few minutes at a time. In 1962, the University established its Computer Science Center, led by Werner Rheinboldt, to consolidate campus research and to offer the first computer science courses. Soon, transistors and integrated circuits transformed computing, creating machines that were ever faster and cheaper. In 1973, the Center created a separate Department of Computer Science that offered undergraduate and graduate degrees. Computer technology soared in the 1980s with the introduction of chip technology and personal computers, the increased use of telephone lines, and the beginning of the Internet. By the end of the decade, the Department of Computer Science was one of the largest on campus, with over fifty-five full-time faculty offering degrees to 600 majors each year, along with thirty M.S. degrees and ten Ph.D.s. It generally ranked among the top ten such programs in the country.

The success of the Computer Science Center and the Department of

Aspiring in the 1980s

Computer Science pushed the University toward the forefront in providing hardware and software to faculty in other departments and providing technicians to help the faculty adapt. It was a boon to research, a stimulus to new ways of thinking.

The world grasped quickly enough the social impact of computers—an explosion of information that transformed the physical sciences, biology, medicine, business management, engineering, even philosophy. Knowledge, rather than energy, powered the economy, vastly boosting it and creating a global economy. Computers also compromised privacy, disenfranchised the non-user, and revolutionized war. We will long be analyzing the gains from the new technology, and possibly the losses.

Business especially felt the computer revolution, and the number of students studying business soared even beyond computer science. The College of Business and Management that had once trained bookkeepers and secretaries was suddenly, in the 1980s, College Park's most popular field for majors. To limit enrollment, the College established the highest admission standards for any major in the University. Still more prestigious as an entry into the business world was the Master of Business Administration degree—1,450 admission applications in 1990 for the 266 openings. The salaries that graduates received explained the popularity of the programs. A part-time, off-campus MBA program brought in huge revenues that enhanced other programs in the college.

Engineering was almost as popular, with its own promise of high-paying employment and its own highly restrictive admission standards. Its innovative dean, George E. Dieter, held undergraduate enrollment steady, but he added twenty-five new faculty positions, obtained a more than tenfold increase in research grants, and extended the program to the University's campus in Baltimore County. Engineering, more than any program since Agricultural Extension in the 1890s, reached beyond the campus. Its Engineering Research Center worked with Maryland high-tech companies to develop new technologies. Its Systems Research Center helped design information systems and automation for established companies. Its Board of Visitors asked the state's ablest engineers and CEOs for advice, and, incidentally, accepted their contributions to facilitate fulfilling that advice.

Rita Colwell, a dynamic professor of microbiology who eventually headed the National Science Foundation, exemplified the new academic entrepreneurship with the creation of a Center for Environmental and Estuarine Studies (1973) and then a Maryland Biotechnology Institute (1983). The centers collected federal money for environmental research,

135

state money for research into economic development, and corporate money for new techniques and products. Each center eventually had an annual budget of over $30 million. Each eventually spun off from College Park to become independent research units of the University of Maryland System.

Other programs also grew, especially at the graduate level. The School of Public Affairs prospered, mostly collecting grants and offering advice to government agencies. The University established a new joint program with the state of Virginia for veterinary medicine. Criminology grew; the biological sciences expanded. Almost every growing program of the 1980s was vocational, offering training for particular occupations. The basic sciences, the social sciences, the humanities, and the arts, still claimed to be the heart of the University, but the students, the money, and even the prestige were moving elsewhere.

EXPECTATIONS

The University looked optimistically forward through the 1980s, enjoying its newfound success but embracing it as merely prelude to something more. The main visionary was the University's president, John Toll. He was a born cheerleader, demanding that the University become one of the top institutions in the country.

The first attempt to be specific about attaining excellence was a failure. Toll employed a superannuated Minnesota educator, Malcolm Moos, to define excellence and show the way, and Moos recommended that Maryland curtail much that already existed in College Park in order to create a new university, located in Baltimore, presumably to enhance or rival Johns Hopkins. Nobody paid much attention or bothered to notice Moos's other ideas about promoting research and public service.

A larger initiative came from Governor Harry Hughes, prompted by Toll, but excited by awareness of higher education's stimulus to Silicon Valley and the California economy. Hughes appointed a Commission on Excellence in Higher Education. Its report, presented in 1987, called for a state bureaucracy to assume control over all of higher education and for College Park to become the center for excellence and research. No longer was success for College Park merely the self-interest of the institution; it had become the self-interest of the state. College Park administrators and faculty feared the report's call for control but liked its call for excellence.

Before Hughes could take action, William Donald Schaefer became governor, with his own agenda for higher education. He particularly liked the idea of tight control and approved of excellence so long as it was a monument to himself, but he wanted development to center in Baltimore. President Toll jumped in. Instead of creating a new bureaucracy, he would personally serve as chancellor for all the state's institutions. He would serve with a single superboard of regents, and, he strongly implied, he would please Baltimore.

Schaefer and Toll were allied; College Park believed its eminence was threatened. Slaughter, bruised enough in the Bias affair, held back, but his vice presidents and deans fought vigorously, appealing directly to members of the General Assembly, the regents, and the newspapers. The General Assembly in 1988 established a compromise: (1) the long-established, mostly advisory State Board for Higher Education would be transformed into a more powerful Maryland Higher Education Commission; (2) Toll and a superboard would manage the five campuses of the University (College Park, University College, Baltimore, Baltimore County, and the Eastern Shore) plus six state colleges (Baltimore, Bowie, Coppin, Frostburg, Salisbury, Towson); and (3) College Park would have "flagship" status, a promise of preeminence. The 1988 settlement also changed the name of the head of the University System from president to chancellor; it changed the name of the campus heads from chancellor to president.

College Park had won; its future as a major institution was assured as never before. There were, however, short-term prices to pay. The struggle cost Slaughter his job. The Bias affair, plus the tension with Toll, was exhausting; he decided that he would be happier at a small college in California. The struggle also cost Toll his job. He looked too much like an empire builder, College Park believed he had been willing to sell them out, the regents were impatient with his over-eagerness to please everybody, and Schaefer felt loyalty to no one. Toll later became president of Washington College, an elite private college on the Eastern Shore, and he was a great success there.

The longer-term results of the shake-up were bright for College Park. Slaughter's successor was William E. Kirwan, whose energy and enthusiasm for the University inspired everyone around him. Toll's successor, after a brief interim, was Donald Langenberg, who was usually able to outmaneuver the Maryland Higher Education Commission above him and was generally willing for College Park to lead his motley pack. Schaefer was rather proud of his creation and usually generous with expanding budgets, and Schaefer's successor was Parris Glendening, a College Park professor who could hardly do enough for his former employers.

William English Kirwan—everyone called him Brit from his middle

86. William E. Kirwan, President from 1988 to 1998, Chancellor of the University System 2002 to present.

name—would, as his successes mounted, become the most popular president the University had ever had. He was the son of a university president at the University of Kentucky, and he rose through the ranks at Maryland—assistant professor of mathematics in 1964, then professor, chair, provost, acting president for a year, then president in 1989. Charming and warm, his enthusiasm for the University was boundless.

Kirwan gave people confidence and pride in their recent progress—the harmony, the flagship designation, the rising budgets and admission standards, the successes of diversity, the modernized curriculum. That was just the beginning. Kirwan promised that Maryland would be evermore egalitarian and more elite, that twenty of its programs would rank among the best in the nation, that the University would reinvigorate the state's economy and the well-being of its people. Faculty liked the message; Governor Schaefer and the General Assembly also liked it. Students and the public had everything to gain in the promises. Within the new University System, President Kirwan of College Park was the largest presence. The Chancellor and the other campus presidents had more to gain by hanging onto his coattails than by uniting against him.

Kirwan, with a dozen committees, drafted an Enhancement Plan that breathlessly measured College Park against five of the country's best state universities—California at Berkeley, California at Los Angeles, Michigan, Minnesota, and North Carolina. Wherever Maryland lagged, there was the challenge to catch up. Salaries, facilities, student selectivity, public outreach—there was much to do. It would cost an additional $30 million a year for the next five years, 125 new faculty, 650 new staff.

The General Assembly was not dismayed; it had asked for the plan. The initiative for a great university was coming not just from campus ambition but from the public and from politics. Appropriations to College Park rose nicely in 1989 and 1990, then paused for recession in the early 1990s, then rose again. "These are magical days at College Park," Kirwan liked to say. Even if the Enhancement Plan was overdone, the future belonged to the University as never before.

CHAPTER XI

The University Triumphant

The 1990s was a golden time for America, more especially for higher education, and most of all for the University of Maryland. For the country, there was unchallenged power and soaring growth. For higher education, the universities were knowledge factories in a knowledge-based economy; never before had they touched so many and been held in such high esteem. For the University of Maryland, the 1990s brought an enthusiastic administration, a friendly governor, ever better students, and ever expanding programs of research and public service. Maryland delighted in the new game that the major universities were playing—ranking itself against the best in the quality and performance of its students, in its research contributions, and in its services to the public.

Everything was getting better for universities, at least as long as everything was getting better for the economy. Many universities, like Maryland, began to worry as the new century began that they had become too dependent on rising tuition, on research grants, and on gifts from their admiring supporters.

KIRWAN, MOTE, AND THE RANKINGS GAME

For College Park, President Toll began the talk about being one of the best universities anywhere; President Kirwan made drumbeat references to national rankings, and his successor, President C. D. Mote, Jr., escalated the rhetoric still more. Talk moved toward reality.

The 1990s began with a brief recession that ironically served the university almost as nicely as prosperity. Kirwan and his vice president, J. Robert Dorfman, seized the opportunity to review all academic programs in order to eliminate the weak ones.

Kirwan and Dorfman knew that initiative had to come from below.

Faculty committees scrutinized each program for its quality and its social utility. The Campus Senate, the administrators, and the regents approved the recommendations.

The modernization eliminated entirely the College of Home Economics, despite its camouflage a few years earlier as a College of Human Ecology. Women no longer needed cooking, sewing, and homemaking as academic disciplines. Remnants of the program, such as nutrition and textiles, moved to other departments. Curriculum reform also ended Departments of Agricultural Education (for extension agents), Industrial Education (for shop teachers), Recreation (for park supervisors), Radio-Television-Film (mainly for technicians), and Urban Studies (absorbed into Architecture). Kirwan claimed that ending these programs saved almost $3 million annually, although in fact the students and the tenured faculty had to be accommodated elsewhere. More important was better education for a higher level of public service. Few conspicuous weak spots remained in the curriculum; not many institutions could say as much. A similar effort to identify and eliminate weak graduate programs mostly failed, except for a few combinations of programs; the faculty lobbies were too strong.

Kirwan's enthusiasm and graciousness warmed students, faculty, alumni, and the public, and he in turn basked in acclaim. Always he was there—before the entering classes, meeting with the Campus Senate, at commencement, before alumni groups, especially before legislative committees—always with the same message, how much the University had progressed since the year before, how it was poised for more. Kirwan truly believed, as few before him had, that teaching, research, and service

87. The Terrapin, called Testudo. Rub the nose for good luck.

really complemented each other, that one did not proceed at the expense of the other.

He encouraged the faculty and the Campus Senate to develop a multitude of strategic plans for moving ahead; he organized a Board of Visitors comprised of distinguished alumni and friends of the campus who might offer advice and further support; and he created a Terrapin Pride Day, when students and faculty descended on Annapolis to express their views on the University's needs.

Kirwan's greatest ally was Parris Glendening, Associate Professor of Government at College Park, on leave as Governor of Maryland. The powerful president of the State Senate, Thomas V. "Mike" Miller, a College Park graduate, was equally supportive. All members of the General Assembly and members of Maryland's Congressional delegation and their families were always welcome in Kirwan's box at football and basketball games.

Governor Glendening was from humble origins; education had been his path to success and was one of the main themes of his administration. For the public schools, he built or refurbished almost half the classrooms in the state and provided major boosts for teacher salaries. Maryland claimed the greatest rise in high school graduation rates in the country, and Glendening legislation provided generous new state aid for needy graduates who went on to college. Money for higher education was plentiful as never before, and especially for College Park. Glendening eagerly embraced the University's drive for national eminence, its claim for special faculty ratios and salaries for research, and its new programs for state service. State surpluses, especially in the late 1990s, went often for new University buildings. Glendening's boasts about the University's progress matched those of its presidents. The General Assembly and the newspapers joined the chorus of approbation.

In 1998, however, Kirwan left to become president of Ohio State University. Good presidents stay on and on; great ones know when to leave. Kirwan departed with a plea for more state funding. Marylanders wept at his departure and took the occasion to celebrate his achievements. After four years in Ohio, where he was again successful, Kirwan returned to Maryland as Chancellor of the University System. His departure from Maryland, however, provided a new beginning, fresh enthusiasm.

The new president was Clayton Daniel Mote, Jr.—Dan—formerly a vice chancellor at the University of California, Berkeley, which was by every measure the nation's best state university. Mote had been an outstanding teacher who believed in undergraduate education; he was a noted

88. Clayton Daniel Mote, Jr., President 1998-present.

research scientist-inventor of new kinds of industrial saws and new kinds of ski equipment—and chair of the Department of Mechanical Engineering, which ranked as the best such department anywhere. In mid-career, Mote became Berkeley's voice to the outside world, promoting research and government relations, and raising $800 million in gifts. People expected him to become Berkeley's chancellor, but the timing was wrong. Instead, savvy, smooth and strong, he became Maryland's president, Maryland's voice to the world. For his academic provost, he selected College Park's Dean of Engineering, William W. Destler.

"Greatness is not our goal, it is our destiny," said Mote. Even more than Toll or Kirwan, he wanted to measure College Park against its competition. Be like Berkeley, be great in everything—in the ranking of each department and each student service, the SAT scores of entering students, the placement of graduates, the number of faculty elected to the national academies, research grants won, gifts obtained. Each ranking must improve each year. New logos and slogans appeared, "Bold Vision, Bright Future," "Momentum," "Zoom," "Fear the Turtle." Maryland was headed for the top, and the world needed to know about it. Campus eminence: that was the starting point for every decision.

The University Triumphant

All universities were into the rankings game; it was the academic vogue of the 1990s, but Maryland particularly liked the game because it was moving up, although never as rapidly as it believed was its due. The most elaborate formula for institutional ranking was the annual listing published by *U.S. News and World Report.* The formula emphasized the opinions of academic officers at rival institutions, but also considered admission standards, retention and graduation rates, faculty ratios and salaries, expenditures for student services, and alumni loyalty. The rankings were not definitive, for institutions differed in mission, offerings and costs, but they were suggestive.

Rankings

Source: *Chronicle for Higher Education,* August 27, 2004

Maryland and Other States:

2nd in highest percentage of population with graduate degrees, 13.4 %, (after Massachusetts).

4th in highest per capita personal income, $37,331, (after Connecticut, Massachusetts, New Jersey).

4th highest percent minority population, 36%, (after California, Mississippi, Louisiana).

10th highest proportion of adults who attended college, 57%, (after Utah, Colorado, Washington, Alaska, Minnesota, Oregon, New Hampshire, Connecticut, Massachusetts).

17th in per capita support for higher education, $238, (after Wyoming, New Mexico, Alaska, North Dakota, North Carolina, Nebraska, Minnesota, California, Mississippi, Kentucky, Kansas, Iowa, Alabama, Utah, Texas, Delaware).

UMCP and Other State Institutions:

9th most foreign students, 3,711 in 2002, (14th among all institutions, public and private).

13th most earned doctorates, 421 in 2002, (16th among all).

17th in total research grants, $353 million in 2002, (31st among all).

19th most freshman merit scholars, 49 in 2003, (42 among all).

18th *U.S. News,* "Best National Universities" (not available among all).

21st total enrollment, 34,160 in 2001, (27th among all).

30th Library Holdings, 3,017,000, (48th among all).

Maryland in 2005 ranked 18th among the 162 publicly supported universities in the country (up from 22nd in 1999, down from 17th in 2004). Six of those above it in 2005 were in California; others were Virginia,

Michigan, North Carolina, William and Mary, Wisconsin, Georgia Tech, Illinois, Texas, Penn State, Washington, and Florida. About thirty private universities ranked higher. Maryland scored above its rank in evaluation by peer institutions, in admission standards, freshman retention, and faculty salaries; it fell below its rank in class size, graduation rate, and alumni loyalty.

Each field within the University earned a ranking, and, although fields were seldom exactly comparable from one institution to another, the ranking in most fields was clear. In 2005, Maryland programs ranked among the top twenty in public *or* private institutions included the A. James Clark School of Engineering (especially its Aerospace and Electrical Engineering programs); College of Education (especially its graduate programs in Counseling, Higher Education Administration, Educational Psychology, Educational Policy, Elementary and Secondary Education, and Special Education programs); Robert H. Smith School of Business graduate programs in Supply Logistics, Entrepreneurship, Management, and part-time MBA; the College of Public Affairs; and in other colleges, the departments of Computer Science, Physics, Mathematics, Applied Mathematics, and Criminology.

Particular programs earned their ranking mainly through research productivity, and in most fields, that productivity came primarily through research grants from government and business. In 2002, Maryland was receiving $353 million in grants, ranking 17th among all state universities. The grants were concentrated in certain fields, but they averaged $229,800 each year for every tenure or tenure-track faculty member. The money went mainly for equipment, for graduate student research assistantships, or for faculty release time. Moving the University ahead in grants and rankings, getting more programs into the top twenty: that was the challenge. Mostly people liked the game. State pride was on the line. There were rewards for the winners.

THE STUDENTS EARNEST

The greatest change at the University of Maryland in the 1990s was the rise of student quality and the enrichment of the student experience. There were measures for these things too, and these were the rankings that were rising most rapidly. In standards for admission, value for tuition paid, honors programs, cultural diversity, and living arrangements, College Park generally ranked as one of the top ten state universities in the country. Student enrollment held steady during the decade, around 33,200, one of the country's thirty largest campuses; minority enrollment (African-

The University Triumphant

American, Asian, Hispanic, Native American) rose from 21 to 28.6 percent; foreign enrollment from 7 to 8.5 percent; graduate enrollment remained about 25 percent. Men remained at about 52 percent of the total, about the same at the undergraduate and graduate level. Size of the student population was more problem than asset, but there were ways to promote communities.

Standards for admission kept rising, because the number of admissions held firm while the college-attending population rose and the University's stature increased. From 1990 to 2004, the median SAT score for the top 75 percent of freshman admissions—the most common comparative admission measure for colleges—rose from 1180 to 1340 (down from 1350 in 2002). The high school grade point average for entering freshmen rose from 3.00 to 3.85, and by 2004, 56 percent of the entering freshmen finished in the top ten percent of their high school class.

For entering freshmen, Maryland had evolved from an overwhelmingly commuter school to a primarily residential one. By 2004, at least 90 percent of the incoming freshmen lived on campus, although many moved off-campus in their later years. Residence facilities were adequate to nearly luxurious, depending on price; students could have singles, doubles, or suites, with or without living rooms and kitchenettes, on floors segregated by sex or mixed. The distinction between campus and private housing blurred, for commercial operators built, leased, or operated campus facilities.

The main features of undergraduate life, however, were new living-learning arrangements. At least fifteen programs brought students together. University Honors, a program for students ranking highest on entrance examinations, expanded all of its offerings—residence facilities, freshman honors seminars, honors versions of regular courses, and specially assigned mentors and seminars for majors. The Gemstone Program brought together teams of about fifteen students focused on a particular problem (solar energy, automobile pollution, biological terrorism, disarmament, poverty); each team took numerous courses together, and, after four years, the team produced a book-length thesis.

There was a College Park Scholars Program, available by invitation only, a two-year, living-learning program arranged around twelve subject areas, in which students took similar courses. The Beyond-the-Classroom Program emphasized internship work in off-campus organizations. The Language House allowed students majoring in a particular language to live and take seminars together, frequently with international students; the Jimenez-Porter Writers House was for prospective writers; the Hinman CEO Program was for aspiring business entrepreneurs. Global Communities and Study Abroad Programs were for students with international interests. CIVICUS was for students interested in government and public service. Most students entered a program of this sort, even if many of the senior faculty, holding to an older order, shunned them.

Ira Berlin, the Dean for Undergraduate Studies who initiated many of these programs, noted that the University of Maryland was making the big store small, creating fine boutiques. In 2003, *U.S. News and World Report* ranked "The First Year Experience" at Maryland as twelfth in the country, below Princeton and Harvard, ahead of Yale and Dartmouth, far ahead of Johns Hopkins and Virginia.

89. The mall and the traffic circle.

The University Triumphant

A remaining problem for most students—a big problem—was money. By 2001, more than half of the undergraduates had part-time jobs; more than 40 percent reported worry about their expenses; and many of the dropouts departed for economic reasons. State appropriations to the University rose 47 percent from 1990 to 2004, but expenses for in-state students rose 105 percent, from $6,594 for tuition, fees, room and board, to $13,506.

Student loans and scholarships were reasonably plentiful for the extremely needy or extremely able, but this applied to a very few. According to figures from the Undergraduate Admissions Office, student loans in the fall of 2003, if averaged among all undergraduates, was about $3,750 each year, mostly from the federal government. On average, for a four-year student, this was a debt of about $15,000 after graduation. Student scholarships based on need, averaged among all undergraduates, amounted to about $950, coming from federal, state, and private sources. Student scholarships based on ability (including athletic ability), averaged about $1,230, coming from private gifts and from the state. In total, the average incoming student was paying $13,506 and was receiving $5,930 in loans and scholarships. This was not bad by national standards; Maryland ranked above average in most-for-the-money rankings. Still, paying for college was a big problem, and a worsening one, and it hung there, like the problem of big-time athletics.

Student services were abundant, mostly paid for with student fees: superb recreation facilities, an ever-expanding student union, orientation, counseling, math-reading-writing-computer clinics, library services, computer services, chapel services, disability services, infirmary service (with free condoms, in all colors), publications, bookstores, career center, alumni facilities, parking facilities (for an extra fee), shuttle bus services, and the list goes on. Each maintained a bureaucracy, generally of dedicated former students.

The student mood of the 1990s—more than in any period of the University's history—was almost everything that the parents of students might have wanted. Above all, students were serious, career-oriented. They worried about college costs and about the future, but they were cheerful, without angst or anger, with a balanced concern for studies, social life, and athletics. Adolescent cynicism and dogmatism were things of the past. The only political dogma was toleration, "Political Correctness." Of course, there were misfits and exceptions—occasional sports rallies got out of hand and sports cheers were notoriously vulgar—but seldom before had the mainstream been so well-defined, mature, and moderate.

Fads and fashions were shallow. Men's clothes were sometimes a size too large, women's sometimes a size too small. Students wore jeans, shirts with slogans, expensive athletic shoes or inexpensive flip-flops, and most of them seemed to be carrying backpacks and cell phones. A few wore tattoos; women often bared their midriffs and sometimes wore navel rings. None of the styles were particularly collegiate; maybe campus life had merged with the world beyond.

A student affairs officer in 2003 counted 422 student organizations: 74 dedicated to minority or international identity (clubs representing 26 nationalities); 71 for academic interests (within most academic departments); 51 for sports and hobbies; 48 honoraries (faculty and students liked to congratulate themselves); 36 political; 27 religious; 25 fraternities; 24 volunteer and service; 18 sororities; and 48 unclassifiable. Athletics kept up with the pace of high rankings and sometimes led the way. The Athletic Director was now a woman, Debbie Yow, and she was pushing the national athletic associations toward tighter control over players. The basketball coach, Gary Williams, handsome and intense, a College Park graduate, sent seven teams to the final sixteen in the national playoffs. In 2002, his team won the national championship, and he was the nation's Coach of the Year. In 2004, the team won the Atlantic Coast Conference championship. College Park was greatly pleased with the victories; sports writers and fans were ecstatic. The football coach, Ralph Friedgen, huge and happy, another College Park graduate, also won a national Coach of the Year award and sent teams to the Orange Bowl (2001), Peach Bowl (2002), and Gator Bowl (2003). Other teams distinguished themselves; women's lacrosse won eight national championships. In 2002, *U.S. News*—using a formula that included team victories, number of sports, gender equity, absence of abuses, and player graduation rate—ranked Maryland among the top twenty athletic programs in the country.

THE IDEAS WAFTING

More important than rankings, larger than student life, were the ideas wafting through classrooms and offices. The ideas flowing through our universities are the cutting-edge ideas of our time. Almost every discipline was undergoing change—paradigm shifts, people liked to say—toward an increasing emphasis on the complexity of the universe. The changes usually had roots early in the century but the new ideas came to prevail in the 1980s and 1990s, touching every basic discipline. The changes were prominent at College Park, although, like student mood and fashion, they prevailed at most good universities.

90. Ralph Friedgen, Football Coach of the Year, 2001

91. Gary Williams, Basketball Coach of the Year, 2002.

The University of Maryland at College Park, A History

Postmodernism was the popular word for the constellation of new ideas. Generally, it meant a rejection of core reality, absolutes, congruity, essence, theme; it meant embrace of particularity, discontinuity, relativism, multiculturalism, pluralism. The disciplines continued to fragment, with specialists unable to speak a common language even while they shared ways of thinking that overlapped and merged.

The new ideas were sharpest in physics, and that field seemed to lead the way. To physicists, the universe seemed to be composed of bundles of energy, quanta, that were without measure in position or velocity. Phenomena could be patterned or unpatterned, there was little distinction, and the laws of physics were mainly probabilities. Physicists talked of an uncertainty principle. University of Maryland Professor James A. Yorke used the phrase "chaos theory" that spread over the country, first through the sciences but then into the humanities. The universe was infinitely complex; impossible ideas must be taken seriously; order was entangled with chaos. Scholars like Thomas S. Kuhn seemed to argue that scientific law itself was merely a cultural concept.

Computer science was a science unto itself, but its tools and its algorithmic thinking reached into every field. Physics and computer science combined to create the science of space that led to the mystery of black holes. Meteorologists formulated the popular image of chaos and complexity: the whiff of the butterfly's wing on one continent creating the hurricane on another. Historians blamed butterflies for the course of human events.

Pure mathematics that once sought models of the universe made way for nonlinear, computational fields, especially applied mathematics and statistics that sought, not laws, but pattern in an incomprehensible universe. The new mathematics merged into computer science, physics, and engineering; into economics and the social sciences; into business and the professions. Axioms became consistencies.

Chemistry explored the electronic properties of matter, atomic structure, cellular structure, and the essence of living things. Organic chemistry especially expanded; the departments of Chemistry and Biochemistry merged. Chemistry reached into cell biology and molecular genetics, plant science, environmental science, and engineering. Chemists talked of nanotubes and of nanotechnology that would create new materials of vast potential.

The biological sciences burgeoned. For decades, the field lagged at College Park, for biology used to flourish mainly around medical schools, but by the 1980s, campus-wide committees persuaded administrators and legislators that biology was replacing physics as the science of the future. Mote especially pushed biology; Maryland must be excellent in everything. The new department emerged at the cusp of the new thinking: DNA, mapping the human genome, genetic engineering, biotechnology, the ecosystem. Biology, too, reached into the other sciences; new faculty arrived; and the grants poured in.

Psychology turned away from behaviorism, with its theory that behavior alone shapes and defines the mind, into cognitive science and neuroscience. Cognitive psychology examines the way the mind uses language and processes information, the ways people learn, anticipate, make decisions, and make different decisions. Neuroscience studies the pathways of thought through the brain.

Economists moved away from John Maynard Keynes's belief in a rational and manageable economy. They occupied themselves with mathematical modeling of micro-phenomena, such as human choices, and macro-phenomena, such as consumption and growth rates. Economists' interests followed the election returns, or vice-versa, for they expressed an increasing bias toward free markets and free trade, control of the money supply, and supply-side stimulus.

Political scientists lost interest in comparing political systems and searching for the institutions that worked best. They embraced the mathematical models taken from economics and they concentrated on particular issues such as conflict resolution, international negotiation, human rights, affirmative action, and campaign contributions. Government needed bureaucrats trained in whatever specialty. Almost any faculty member could find a problem with a solution that a government bureau or foundation wanted to support.

Sociology, finally bored with the study of social classes, turned to demography and to specific problems of poverty, deviance, and family stability. Anthropologists and archeologists embraced the ideas of Clifford Geertz, that cultures are patterns of behavior and mentality, all created by context and circumstance, all very different and very equal.

In the humanities, new ways of thinking were strikingly related to those in the sciences. The study of history moved away from story and theme (these were distortions), away even from events (they were inexplicable, random), away from synthesis and generalization. Instead, reveling in the complexity, contingency, and even the unknowability of the past, historians concentrated on the particularities of social and cultural history—how ordinary people thought and felt, and how elemental concerns about race, status, and gender shaped their lives. Emphasis on the United

States and Western Civilization broadened into new focus on Asia, Africa, and Latin America.

Literature and language departments turned away from the "canon"—meaning the famous and recognized writers. Jacques Derrida argued that writers were only a mass of biases, like our own. Instead, scholars should concentrate on ways in which the written word was perceived; scholars should listen to the voices from popular culture, and especially from women, minorities, and the oppressed. The mere esthetics of novels or poems was elitist; a higher concern was the popular preoccupation with matters of race, class, and gender.

The field of philosophy moved away from metaphysics and definitions, away from Kant and Hegel. It moved instead toward the new pragmatism of Richard Rorty and John Rawls, toward the everyday problems of morality, human rights, and social justice. An Institute of Philosophy and Public Policy emerged at Maryland to address policy questions in medical ethics, racial identity, environmentalism, globalism. New courses offered a philosophical basis for thinking about the arts, literature, medicine, physics, biology, and human communication.

The booming fields of African-American studies, women's studies, Jewish studies, and area studies all moved away from search for identity, or search for heroes and heroines, or concern with victimization; all evolved toward simple delight in particularity.

The drift in the disciplines toward complexity and particularity, and especially their embrace of ambiguity, probably distanced the academic world from the public. The embrace of ambiguity helped explain the academic leaning toward the left. Still, the accompanying concern with applicability served the public. The basic disciplines were losing students to the professional schools, and the professions were most actively building the bridges from theory to applicability, and from the campus to the world.

THE UNIVERSITY AND THE WORLD BEYOND

The land grant colleges emerged in the 1860s not merely to educate but to promote the agricultural economy, and after half a century, they began to succeed. Now, nearly a century after that, American universities were awakening to their potential for enhancing other segments of society. The state of Maryland was employing at College Park more than three thousand of the world's best minds, not merely to teach, not merely to contemplate the complexities of the universe, but to promote the economy and well-being of people beyond the campus. To be sure, the

The University Triumphant

University had long claimed service as a mission, but, except in agriculture, it was hardly so. Now, however, late in the twentieth century, the state and the campus awakened together to the potential.

The model was Silicon Valley, where scientists at Stanford and California-Berkeley had seemed to be the source of a vast new computer and telecommunication industry. Maryland was eager to keep up. Governors Schaefer and Glendening loved the concept of the University as an engine of the economy. The concept was Schaefer's justification for College Park's flagship status and for the appropriations that followed. The economic engine led to still larger concepts: the University's expertise could address social issues; its artists could invigorate the arts.

At College Park, as in California, the College of Engineering was the leader in reaching aggressively into the business world. Industrial development was overwhelmingly technological, the University possessed the state's most advanced engineering laboratories, and faculty and graduate students were developing an ever-larger portion of the patents for new techniques and products. Faculty members, along with a handful of their best graduate students, were departing to establish their own companies. Star graduates were employing their former professors, utilizing University facilities for further development, and expressing gratitude with endowments.

92. Maryland Day attracted up to 70,000 people.

Major Construction, 1988-2005

1988   A. V. Williams Computer Sciences, $14 million. A. V. Williams is a philanthropist.
Annapolis Dorm, $19.4 million.
Regents Drive Parking Facility, $12.9 million.

1990   McKeldin Library Addition, $30 million.

1990   Surge Building, later Susquehanna, $9.1 million.
Agricultural and Life Sciences, $5.6 million.

1991   Van Munching Hall, Smith School of Business and School of Public Affairs, $30 million. Leo Van Munching was a philanthropist.
Gossett Football Team House, $11.9 million. Barry Gossett is a philanthropist.
Laboratory for Physical Sciences, $11.2 million.

1995   Byrd Stadium Upper Deck, $10.9 million.

1996   Plant Sciences Building, $39.6 million.
Nyumburu Center, $3.3 million. Nyumburu means Freedom House.

1997   Stadium Drive Parking Facility, $12.3 million.

1998   Campus Recreation Center, $40 million.
Technology Advancement Center, $6.4 million.

1999   Golf Course Clubhouse, $2.5 million.

2000-2004   University Courtyard Apartments, leased, $195.5 million.

2001   Clarice Smith Performing Arts Center, $130 million. Clarice Smith is a philanthropist.

2001-2004   South Campus Commons, leased, $195.5 million.

2002   Van Munching Hall addition, $38 million.
Comcast Center, $125 million.
Computer Science Instructional Center, $9.7 million.

2003   Research Greenhouses, $16 million.
Mowatt Lane Parking Facility, $20 million.

2004   Jeong Kim Engineering Building, $56 million. Jeong Kim is a philanthropist.

2005   Samuel Riggs IV Alumni Center, $20 million. Samuel Riggs is a philanthropist.

2006   Biological Sciences Research Building, $56 million.

State and University officials watched the movement with delight; everyone gained; barriers between government, education, and business faded. Grants poured in, especially for research that promised economic advancement, especially from the federal government. The University established a Technology Advancement Program offering space and support services for start-up companies, a Technology Extension Service that helped established companies solve technical problems, and a Maryland Industrial

The University Triumphant

Partnerships program provided joint development and financing of new industries. There were campus offices for securing patents, obtaining capital, and training employees. The programs mostly paid for themselves, education benefited, the state and national economy gained.

Engineering's boost to the economy was a two-way street. The college established its own Board of Visitors composed of the state's most prominent engineers to lobby for support. A college alumnus, A. James Clark, gave $15 million, and the college renamed itself. Another alumnus, Jeong Kim, gave $5 million, and the college named a building for him.

The College of Business and Management was the other leader in reaching to the world beyond. Except for computer science and engineering, the College of Business was growing faster in size and prestige than any unit in the University. It was an age of entrepreneurship, with grants from government to promote business, grants from business to explore business frontiers, and gifts from business to celebrate success. The College received $15 million from Robert H. Smith and adopted his name; it received $14 million from Leo Van Munching and named its building after him. A price list was available. People could put their name on endowed chairs, a classroom, or a scholarship—a noble philanthropy, a nice memorial, good for everybody. Firms doing business with the University were especially philanthropic.

The Robert H. Smith School of Business touched almost every business in Maryland and the Washington, D.C. area. Its Dingman Center for Entrepreneurship, endowed with an $8 million gift, offered counseling to businesses on matters of management, finance, computer systems, and marketing. The Maryland Small Business Development Center, distantly related to the Robert H. Smith School, facilitated contacts and provided training courses. Other agencies conducted surveys or provided special research reports.

The University's Center for Institutional Reform and the Informal Sector, a spin-off from the Department of Economics, supervised the expenditure of over $100 million in federal funds for the promotion of free markets, first in the former Soviet Union, ultimately in over sixty countries around the world. The Center for the Advanced Study of Languages, established jointly with the National Security Agency, promoted a sympathetic understanding of the world, and perhaps an American reach over the globe as well.

The College of Agriculture, once the entire institution, diffused into natural resources, dietetics, environmental science, and landscape architecture. The College of Education reached deeply into the public schools, but its faculty made their names mainly through publication. The same was true for the School of Architecture and the College of Health and Human Performance. The Philip Merrill College of Journalism, so named after a $10 million gift from a local publisher, employed some of the great voices from the world's capital nearby, and probably helped shape that voice.

College Park sponsored at least 106 "centers," 19 "consortia," 15 "institutes," and at least 30 other bureaus and associations—usually funded by grants, closely linked with faculty research and graduate training, and usually working with groups beyond the campus. Every week, in most departments, someone from another university or from beyond academe visited to deliver a lecture, and every week most departments sent a lecturer elsewhere. The University acquired a research park, located near the College Park Metro stop, which was leased to corporations and government agencies that established links with campus research. On the other side of the campus, the United States National Archives—built on University property—established ties with campus departments. The College Park campus established a Dean for Continuing and Extended Education with a mostly self-supporting program that offered credit or noncredit education to business or public groups, designed to their order.

93. The Robert H. Smith School of Business, Van Munching Hall.

The University Triumphant

The University's outreach was more than economic and political, for the biggest outreach initiatives were in the arts and athletics.

The Clarice Smith Performing Arts Center was one of the largest structures on the campus. The University had wanted a music building. Area enthusiasts, then President Kirwan, then Governor Schaefer began to imagine more—a suburban center as rival or successor to Washington's Kennedy Center. Money came from the state and county, from student fees, philanthropy, and the promise of ticket sales. Clarice Smith, wife of Robert Smith, who had endowed and named the College of Business, gave $15 million; altogether the building cost $130 million. The handsome structure, completed in 2001, was essentially ten buildings linked along a winding arcade—a concert hall, recital hall, four theatres, a library, nearly eighty rooms for classes and rehearsals, along with office wings for the School of Music and Departments of Dance and Theatre.

Build it, and they will come. The response was overwhelming, 1,000 performances a year, most filled nearly to capacity, many attending who had seldom patronized the arts before. All performances were linked to the University's instructional programs, and professional performers relished the association. The educational programs in the arts burgeoned. No realistic planner would have promoted such a vast scheme for the University, and yet it worked.

Athletics was another kind of public service. Mention the University of Maryland anywhere in America, and people knew about its athletic programs. Thousands attended the games, sometimes millions watched on television. At Byrd Stadium, there were new decks, boxes, and plush seats for big donors. The Comcast Center for basketball opened in 2002, at a cost of $130 million, one of the finest sports arenas in the world: weight rooms, trophy rooms, entire suites for coaches, for academic tutors, fund raisers, schedulers, and especially public relations. Comcast, a telecommunications company, outmaneuvered Enron for the naming rights.

Athletics was part of the University triumphant, maybe rampant in the world. Sportswriters liked to say, in sportswriter language, that athletics was a metaphor for life—striving, winning, and losing. Certainly it was celebration of the body—strength, speed, agility, endurance. It was celebration of what the coaches called character—discipline, training, striving, winning. It provided a focus for human impulses—crowds united in their cheers, ordinary people yearning for heroes, society's need for rules and fair play, humanity's need for the decisiveness of victory or defeat. The public loved the University for its teams, and their excellence outshone most of the lingering questions about athletics. Commercialization?

94. Comcast Center Arena.

95. Byrd Stadium, 2003.

The University Triumphant

The free market worked. Exploitation of players? The players didn't think so. The University loomed large. Fear the Turtle.

THE PUBLIC-PRIVATE UNIVERSITY

The new century began badly—corporate scandal, terrorism, indecisive wars, a stalled economy. Maryland's new governor, Robert L. Ehrlich, a Princeton graduate, was not especially friendly; his first two budgets, for 2003 and 2004, provided for a combined 15 percent cutback in state funding for College Park, and the appropriation for 2005 was identical to the year before. The University made up some of its losses by freezing salaries, curtailing services, and by still more tuition increases. To be sure, higher education was suffering about equally in other states. The climate for higher education was different.

As we gain perspective on the times in which we are living, the beginning of the new century may mark the beginning of a new chapter for the University and for all higher education. The theme of the chapter will almost certainly be the continuing rise of the importance of universities, but it may also mark a waning of public support, a waning of interest in rankings, and a growing similarity between public and private institutions. These are not yet the established themes, but there are feints in these directions.

The decline in the proportion of the University's funding from the state was dramatic: in 1990 the state was providing 43 percent of the University's operating revenue, and in 2004 the state's contribution had fallen to 27 percent.

University Revenue, 1990-2005

Revenue Source	1990 Dollars (millions)	1990 Percent of Budget	2005 Dollars (millions)	2005 Percent of Budget
State Appropriation	225	43	310	27
Tuition, Fees	99	19	315	28
Research Grants & Contracts	84	16	256	22
Gifts	17	3	56	5
Room, Board, Ticket Sales, etc.	93	18	206	18
Total Budget (millions)	519		1,143	

Much of the explanation for the relative decline in state support lay in the extraordinary rise in research grants and private gifts. The University's greatest success in the 1990s had been its direct partnership with corporations and with the public, and, as usually happens in history, success evoked a challenge, for taxpayers were beginning to ask the University to depend on its new revenues.

Another explanation for the relative decline in state support lay in the twenty-first century's trend toward smaller government, lower taxes, and privatization of services. The public's traditional view, at least since World War II, had been that state expenditures for higher education benefited everyone, that the state's investment had a multiplier effect in promoting the state's economy and well-being. The new argument was that minimum taxes were a higher priority, that those who gained most of the benefits from education and services should pay most of the costs.

Mainly, the costs fell on the students. For almost a century, from the 1890s to the 1990s, most students could obtain a college education by working part-time and taking an extra year for their degree, but now that opportunity was narrowing. For many students, the cost of attending the state university was as out-of-sight as it had been more than a century before. Briefly, the state considered caps on the tuition that state institutions might charge. Instead, the state—and the federal government as well—expanded slightly its student loans and tuition vouchers. The vouchers tended to equalize institutions, for they were equally good at private and state universities and at community colleges.

The major public and private universities were growing increasingly similar—especially in their missions of research and service beyond the campus. Once, the state university was mainly concerned with develop-

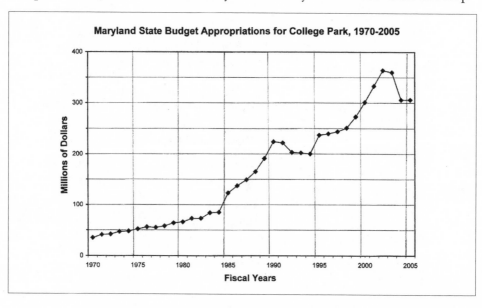

Maryland State Budget Appropriations for College Park, 1970-2005

ing all students to their highest potential, but it increasingly became more concerned with training for those with the highest potential for making a contribution. The public and private universities were in increasing competition for research grants, rankings, and the same faculty and students.

Perhaps, too, universities were becoming more like business corporations, competing for investments, competing for efficiency and productivity, their presidents like CEOs, their employees like partners in a firm or a corporate labor force. In 2001, the College Park clerical staff and maintenance workers voted 920 to 188 to join the American Federation of State, County, and Municipal Employees. Unionization probably improved working conditions and job security, but it probably lessened employee loyalty to the University's mission. Graduate teaching assistants talked of unionization, although the faculty hardly considered it.

The public-private partnership—or privatization—was evident as the University leased its dormitories and food services to private contractors, as it bowed to the commercialization of athletics, and as it sold off the names of its buildings and classrooms to private donors. It was evident in the sixteen-story apartment building, University View, just north of the campus, privately owned but designed for students and faculty, and almost a part of the campus. It was hard to say whether M-Square, the planned $500 million research park just east of the campus, was private or public.

The present-day changes within the University are sometimes disconcerting, especially to those who are inclined to look backward. But the changes are probably good. Universities are always changing; this is their strength. Think back, here at College Park, to the aspirations of founders like Charles Calvert in the 1850s, and to builders like Curley Byrd, Wilson Elkins, Johnny Toll, Brit Kirwan and Dan Mote. Always the aspirations and attainments are higher, always the past has been prelude to something better.

Today, near the 150th anniversary of its founding, the University of Maryland at College Park is a home and community for over 9,000 employees and some 34,000 students. It is one of the leading universities in the world, a source of improvement for individuals and progress for society, a font of ideas, understanding, and wisdom. Its past has been worth our efforts, its future worth our aspiration.

Presidents at College Park
(Called Chancellors, 1970-1988)

President	Previous Career	Served	
1. Benjamin Hallowell	Quaker Schoolmaster	1859	1 month
2. Charles Benedict Calvert	Planter	(Acting) 1859-1860	1 year
3. John M. Colby	Schoolmaster	1860-1861	1 year
4. Henry Onderdonk	Quakar Schoolmaster	1861-1864	3 years
5. Nicholas B. Worthington	Journal Editor	(Acting) 1864-1867	3 years
6. Charles L. C. Minor	Captain, CSA	1867-1868	1 year
7. Franklin Buchanan	Admiral, CSA	1868-1869	1 year
8. Samuel Regester	Methodist Preacher	1869-1873	4 years
9. Samuel Jones	Major General, CSA	1873-1875	2 years
10. William H. Parker	Navy Captain, CSA	1875-1882	7 years
11. Augustine J. Smith	Merchant	1883-1887	4 years
12. Allen Dodge	Banker	(Acting) 1887-1888	1 year
13. Henry E. Alvord	Agriculturalist, Univ. Mass.	1888-1892	4 years
14. Richard W. Silvester	Farmer	1892-1912	20 years
15. Thomas H. Spence	Classical Languages	(Acting) 1912-1913	1 year
16. Harry J. Patterson	Agricultural Experiment Station	1913-1917	4 years
17. Albert F. Woods	President, Univ. Minnesota	1917-1926	9 years
18. Raymond A. Pearson	President, Univ. Iowa	1926-1935	9 years
19. Harry Clifton Byrd	Football Coach	1935-1954	19 years
20. Thomas B. Symons	Dean Agriculture	(Acting) 1954	6 months
21. Wilson H. Elkins	President, Texas Western Univ.	1954-1970	16 years
22. Charles E. Bishop	Vice President, Univ. N. Car.	1970-1974	4 years
23. John W. Dorsey	Vice Chancellor	(Acting) 1974-1975	1 year
24. Robert L. Gluckstern	Provost, Univ. Massachusetts	1975-1982	7 years
25. John B. Slaughter	Director, NSF	1982-1988	6 years
26. William E. Kirwan	Provost	1988-1998	9 years
27. Clayton Daniel Mote, Jr.	Vice Chancellor, Cal., Berkeley	1998-	

Chancellors of the University System
(Called Presidents, 1970-1988)

1. Wilson H. Elkins	President, College Park	1970-1978	8 years
2. John S. Toll	President, SUNY, Stony Brook	1978-1989	11 years
3. James A. Norton	President Hiram College	(Acting) 1989-1990	1 year
4. Donald N. Langenberg	Chancellor, Univ. Illinois	1990- 2002	12 years
5. William E. Kirwan	President, Ohio State	2002-	

Photo Credits

1. Enoch Pratt Free Library, Baltimore; 2. College Relations, Washington College, Chestertown; 3. Archives, University of Maryland in Baltimore; 4. Library of Congress, Prints and Photographs; 5. Henry E. Huntington Library, San Marino, California; 6. Riversdale Historical Society; 7. Archives, University of Maryland College Park (hereafter Archives, UMCP); 8. Maryland Historical Society; 9. Library of Congress, Prints and Photographs; 10. Prince George's County Historical Society; 11. Archives, UMCP; 12. Enoch Pratt Free Library; 13-15, Maryland Historical Society; 16. Mrs. Olive Reeder and Craig L. Symonds, *Confederate Admiral* (Naval Institute, Annapolis); 17-20. College Yearbooks, Maryland Media Inc. (hereafter MM); 21. Prince George's County Historical Society; 22. Maryland National Capital Park and Planning, History Division; 23-28. Yearbooks, MM; 29. College Park Aviation Museum; 30-32. Yearbooks, MM; 33. Archives, UMCP; 34-45. Yearbooks, MM; 46. Prince George's County Historical Society; 47. Yearbook, MM; 48. History Department, UMCP; 49. Yearbook, MM; 50. College Park Aviation Museum; 51-53. Yearbooks, MM; 54-56. Archives UMCP; 57-61. Yearbooks, MM; 62. Maryland Historical Society; 63. Yearbooks, MM; 64. Archives, UMCP; 65. Yearbook, MM; 66-68. Yearbooks, MM; 69. Resident Housing Association, UMCP; 70-75. Yearbooks, MM; 76. Archives, UMCP; 77. Yearbook, MM; 78. Maryland Athletics, Media Relations; 79-84. Yearbooks, MM; 85. Maryland Athletics, Media Relations; 86. Archives, UMCP (copyright, UMCP, 1995); 87. Yearbook, MM; 88. Archives, UMCP (copyright, UMCP, 2000); 89. Archives, UMCP (copyright, UMCP, 2002); 90-91. Yearbooks, MM; 92. Archives, UMCP (copyright, UMCP, 2002); 93. Smith School of Business; 94-95. Maryland Athletics, Media Relations; Dust Jacket: Maryland Historical Society.

Index

170

Franklin, Benjamin: 4
Franklin, Thomas: 26
Franklin College: 6
Fraternities: 61, 89, 104, 150
Frederick College: 6
Free University: 103
Freidlin, Mark I.: 129
Fretz, Bruce: 93
Friedgen, Ralph: 150, 151
Frostburg State University: 137

G

G.I. Bill: 77
Gantt, Elizabeth: 129
Gardner, Bruce L.: 129
Gator Bowl: 85, 114, 150
Geertz, Cliford: 153
Gemstone Program: 147
General Research Board: 91
Geology: 21, 118
Georgetown University: 73
Gilbert, James B.: 129
Glee Club: 44
Glendening, Parris: 137, 143, 155
Global Communities Program: 147
Gloeckler, George: 129
Gluckstern, Robert L.: 119-22, 125, 165
Godefroy, Maximilian: 8
Godfather's Gift: 17
Golden ID: 120
Goldhaber, Jacob: 93
Goldsborough, Phillips Lee: 48
Goldsborough, William T.: 16
Goldstein, Irwin L.: 1, 128
Golf Course: 95
Government and Politics, Department of: 76, 121
Grades: 89, 92, 113
Graduate School: 59, 136
Great Depression: 67
Groome, John C.: 16
Gulick, Denny: 93
Gurr, Ted Robert: 129
Gym-Library: 46

H

H. J. Patterson Hall: 74, 75

Haight-Ashbury: 104
Hall of Fame Bowl: 114
Hallowell, Benjamin: 20, 21
Harlan, Louis R.: 129
Harris, Chapin A.: 9
Harvard University: 4, 119, 148
Hatch, William, and Hatch Act: 35
Hayden, Horace H.: 9
Health and Human Performance, College of: 118, 158
Health Service: 149
Henson, Jim: 125
Hicks, Thomas: 25
Higher Education Administration: 146
Hinman CEO Program: 147
History, Department of: 94, 114, 118, 128, 154
Hodos, William: 129
Hoffman, David: 8
Holzapfel Hall: 65, 74
Home Economics, College of: 53, 77, 98, 112, 142
Honors Program: 92, 114, 120
Hook, Elizabeth: 50
Hopkins, Johns: 12, 17
Hornbake Library: 118, 119
Hornbake Plaza: 128
Hornbake, R. Lee: 91
Hughes, Harry: 123, 133, 136
Human Ecology, College of: 142
Human Relations Office: 114
Hunt, Janet: 93
Hyattsville: 48, 116

I

In Loco Parentis: 103
Industrial Education, Department of: 142
Institute for Mechanic Arts: 6
Institute of Philosophy and Public Policy: 154
Institutes: 158
Institutional Reform and the Informal Sector, Center for: 157
Intensive Educational Program: 114
Intercollegiate Athletics, Department of: 120
Interdisciplinary Study: 113
Internships: 114
Irving College: 6

Maryland Higher Education Commission: 137

Maryland Industrial Partnership: 156

Maryland Small Business Development Center: 157

Maryland, State: agriculture in: 31; appropriation to higher education: 1920 to 1954: 67, 71, 74, 80; 1954 to 1990: 90, 122, 133, 134, 139; 1990 to 2005: 149, 161; before 1920: 5, 10, 17, 23, 34, 50, 52; education in: 6; wealth in: 31

Maryland State Agricultural Society: 12

Maryland State College: 53, 84

MaryPIRG: 116

Mathematical and Physical Sciences and Engineering: 112

Mathematics, Department of: 93, 94, 128, 146

Mathias, J. Marshal: 69

May Day: 62

MBA Degree: 135

McKeldin Mall: 74

McKeldin, Theodore: 85, 89, 100

McMillen, Tom: 114

Me Decade: 116

Medicine, College of: 6, 7, 17

Medieval Mercenary Militia: 125

Mencken, H. L.: 71

Mercer Literary Society: 22

Mercer, William N.: 16, 17

Merryman, John: 16

Meteorology: 129

Michigan State University: 17

Microbiology: 74, 135

Middle States Association of Colleges and Secondar: 85

Middleton, William: 17

Military Training: 33

Miller, Gerald Ray: 93

Miller, Thomas V.: 143

Minker, Jack: 128

Minor, Charles L. C.: 32

Minority Students: 114, 146

Mitchell, Parren: 84

Monroe, James: 18

Moos, Malcolm: 136

More, Thomas: 3

Morgan State University: 105

Morrill Hall: 46, 52, 74

Morrill, Justin S.: 28, 30

Mote, Clayton Daniel, Jr.: 1, 141, 143, 153, 163

Mount Hope College: 6

Mount, M. Marie: 53

Mount St. Mary's College: 6

Mount Washington Female College: 6

Multiversity: 133

Murray, Donald: 68

Music, School of: 159

N

Nader, Ralph: 116

Nanotechnology: 152

National Archives: 158

National Collegiate Athletic Association: 131, 133

National Defense Education Act: 87, 90

National Guard: 101, 108, 109

National Institutes of Health: 87

National Science Foundation: 87, 124, 135

National Security Agency: 157

National Youth Administration: 74

Native Americans: 4, 17

Nelson, Arthur: 17

Nemes, Graciela: 128

New Deal: 69, 73

New Left: 105

New Windsor College: 6

New York Times: 69, 83

Newton College: 6

Nice, Harry: 74

Nixon, Richard: 108

Novikov, Serguei: 129

Nyumburu Cultural Center: 114

O

Office of Equal Opportunity: 114

Ohio State University: 143

Old Line: 68, 89

Ollman, Bertram: 121

Olmsted Brothers: 74

Olson, Mancur: 117, 129

Onderdonk, Henry: 26, 28

Orange Bowl: 85, 150

Orientation: 114

175

Turkos, Anne S. K.: 1
Turner, Mark: 129
Turnpike: 14, 18, 37, 50
Tydings, Millard E.: 44, 53, 74, 100

U

U.S. News and World Report: 145, 148
Uncertainty Principle: 152
Undergraduate Studies, Dean for: 113, 128, 148
Unions: 163
United States Bureau of Mines: 74
United States Department Health, Education, Welfar: 111, 114
United States Naval Academy: 6, 32, 39
University Archives: 1
University Boulevard: 74
University College: 81, 100, 111, 137
University Honors: 147
University of California, Berkeley: 101, 105, 139, 143, 155
University of California, Los Angeles: 139
University of Maryland: 1782: 4; 1812 to 1920: 6, 7, 9, 29, 31, 39, 53
University of Maryland, Baltimore County: 100, 111, 135, 137
University of Maryland, College Park: mission: 124, 155, 163; revenue, 1990-2005: 161
University of Maryland System: 136
University of Michigan: 139
University of North Carolina: 111, 139
University of Pennsylvania: 4
University of Virginia: 12, 32
University Relations: 1
University Senate: 93, 106, 108, 112
University View: 163
Upward Bound: 114
Urban Studies: 142

V

Van Bokkelen, Libertus: 29, 56
Van Munching, Leo: 156, 157
Vaux, Charlotte: 50
Veterans: 77
Veterans Administration: 81
Veterinary Medicine: 136

Vietnam: 87, 101, 105, 107, 108, 110

W

Wade, Bob: 132, 133
Walters, William B.: 93
Warfield Commission: 99
Washington College: 4, 137
Washington Medical College: 6
Washington Post: 64, 97
Webb, Richard A.: 129
Weeks, John D.: 129
Weingaertner, Ellie: 93
Weller, Chris: 114
Wellford, Charles F.: 93
Western Maryland College: 53, 73
Wharton, John O.: 16, 17, 22
White, Charles M.: 44
Whittle, Hiram: 84
Williams, Buck: 114
Williams, Ellen D.: 129
Williams, Gary: 150
Wolvin, Andrew: 93
Women: admitted: 50; and Title IX: 120; athletics: 114, 120; equity for: 111; in 1920s: 61, 64
Women's Studies, Department of: 114, 118, 127, 154
Woods, Albert F.: 50, 52, 53, 59, 64, 65, 73
Woodstock: 104
Works Progress Administration: 74
World War I: 41, 52
World War II: 134
Worthington, Nicholas B.: 16
Wright, Wilbur: 50

Y

YMCA: 61, 68
Yorke, James A.: 129, 152
Yow, Deborah: 150

Z

Zimmerman, P. W.: 53
Zoology-Psychology Building: 118, 119
Zwanzig, Robert W.: 129